# AUDUBON
# The Kentucky Years

L. CLARK KEATING

THE UNIVERSITY PRESS OF KENTUCKY

For Richard

Research for The Kentucky Bicentennial Bookshelf
is assisted by a grant from the
National Endowment for the Humanities.
Views expressed in the Bookshelf do not
necessarily represent those of the Endowment.

ISBN: 0-8131-0215-4

Library of Congress Catalog Card Number: 75-38216

Copyright © 1976 by The University Press of Kentucky

A statewide cooperative scholarly publishing agency
serving Berea College, Centre College of Kentucky,
Eastern Kentucky University, Georgetown College,
Kentucky Historical Society, Kentucky State University,
Morehead State University, Murray State University,
Northern Kentucky State College, Transylvania University,
University of Kentucky, University of Louisville, and
Western Kentucky University.

*Editorial and Sales Offices:* Lexington, Kentucky 40506

# Contents

# Preface

WITH THE PASSAGE of the years, interest in John James Audubon and his studies of American wildlife appears to increase. As an ornithologist and colorful personality he has eclipsed all but completely even the most competent of his rivals and predecessors. He is still first in our hearts, and in these days when the world's need to conserve wildlife is universally recognized, his name and achievements are a talisman for us all.

It will come as a shock to many bird lovers to learn that Audubon, whose name has become synonymous with the preservation and conservation of wildlife, was guilty at times of a reckless slaughter of birds and other wild creatures. He reports, for instance, that on one occasion he killed no less than sixty Lapland larkspurs, and he adds with no apparent regret that on the following day his brother-in-law shot six hundred. In our century we find it hard to excuse this wanton destruction of life. The only justification one can offer is to note that in such an action Audubon was neither more nor less than a man of his times. It is some consolation, however, to learn that as an old man the naturalist had changed his attitude radically. He became aware that the indiscriminate killing of birds was making some species rare. It is reported of him that on at least one occasion he summarily refused to let a certain bird be killed for him, even though he needed it for close observation. Because it was rare, he said, he preferred to do without it. This change was characteristic of Audubon. As time went on, he became astonishingly aware of what was happening to America and to the wilderness areas he loved so well. He knew he could not stop the clock nor reverse the trend toward urbanization of the countryside, but he could and did change his own practices. For him, at least, hunting as a sport became a thing of the past.

A rather brief, but highly significant, period of Audubon's life—from 1807 to 1819—was spent in the Commonwealth of Kentucky. It was here that his children were born, here that his avocation as a bird painter developed and flourished, here that the sight of Alexander Wilson's collection of bird paintings probably pointed him in the direction of his life's work. My purpose in these pages is to review these Kentucky years, taking leave of the naturalist only when circumstances led him to leave the state. For detailed treatment of his years as a boy in France and as a young man living at Mill Grove Farm near Philadelphia, as well as of the years of struggle and fame that followed his sojourn in Kentucky, the reader is referred to any one of the excellent studies on the naturalist's career. Preeminent among these are books by Alice Ford, especially her *John James Audubon* (Norman: University of Oklahoma Press, 1964). Also recommended are Alexander B. Adams's *John James Audubon* (New York: Putnam & Sons, 1966), and Francis Hobart Herrick's *Audubon the Naturalist* (New York: Appleton, 1917). Invaluable for this study has been the unpublished master's thesis (University of Kentucky, 1970) of J. D. Book, Jr., *John James Audubon in Kentucky.* Audubon's own autobiographical writings, recently arranged in chronological order by Alice Ford, are the best source of all.

In Kentucky, as in all America, Audubon's memory is still green. The researcher who visits the naturalist's haunts of more than a century and a half ago need but identify himself as a follower of the artist's trail to find all doors open to him. Librarians who were complete strangers a moment ago are eager to pile his table high with books, scrapbooks, and documents. Friends and colleagues who have caught wind of the project, however vaguely, take pleasure in making available all sorts of bits and pieces of information.

This is certainly the proper place to acknowledge with thanks all these kindnesses as well as my indebtedness to all sources. The story has often been told and well told. May this retelling with an almost total emphasis on the Kentucky years embellish rather than detract from the Audubon tradition.

# 1

# JEAN-JACQUES
# AUDUBON

A GREAT DEAL of energy has been expended in attempts to prove that Jean-Jacques Audubon was the lost dauphin of France, spirited out of the country during the Terror, to be brought up by loyal henchmen of the crown. Subsequently, the legend runs, he was sent quietly across the sea to America. There he grew up and finally settled on the frontier, where he always refused to confide in anyone the secret of his royal parentage. Thus the romantic tale, which Audubon did nothing to discourage. He was never frank about his origins and the stories he chose to tell from time to time were not consistent. Little wonder then that romantic biographers saw in this lack of precision a deliberate attempt to mystify. Now, thanks to the accomplishment of recent research, all these legends about Audubon's parentage and place of birth have been laid to rest.

The facts are these. Jean-Jacques Audubon was the son of Lieutenant Jean Audubon of the French navy and Jeanne Rabine, a French woman and fellow passenger of Lieutenant Audubon on a ship bound for the West Indies. The child was born in Les Cayes, Haiti, April 26, 1785, and his mother died November 11 of the same year. The fact that Lieutenant Audubon had a wife in France at the time seems not to have mattered to anyone concerned. Audubon's wife welcomed his illegitimate son, whom she saw for the first time when he was four and one-half years old, and treated him thereafter as her own. It is a matter of record that Jean Audubon and his wife formally adopted Jean-Jacques through court procedure. In later years the naturalist was to say affectionately of Anne Moynet Audubon that she was not a stepmother to him but a mother indeed: "I loved her as if she had been my own mother, and well did she merit my affection." She was, in fact, the only mother he remembered.

Young Audubon was an intense and serious boy who took wholeheartedly to certain studies and as wholeheartedly rejected others. His father's ambition was to make a naval officer of him, but he discovered that the lad had an aversion to both mathematics and navigation; at the end of three years the naval school sent him home. Not surprisingly, while at school he had paid strict attention to draftsmanship, to his French, and to fencing. He also enjoyed his lessons on the flute and the violin and was an apt pupil at freehand drawing. During these years he had already made a small collection of sketches of French birds. Thus by the time he left France at the age of eighteen, he had acquired several of the drawing-room skills of the French naval cadet and had revealed a modest talent for drawing.

Leaving France for the New World was a move all but inevitable for a young man not possessed of military ambitions. The year was 1803 and times were bad. The horrors of the French Revolution had disappeared only to be replaced by the ruthless tactics of Napoleon's recruiting gangs. It seemed, therefore, to Lieutenant Audubon and his wife the better part of valor to send Jean-Jacques safely out of the country. In this connection he bethought himself at once of his friend Miers Fisher, a Quaker lawyer in the United States, and of his own country place in Pennsylvania—a farm he had bought and then leased out. Called Mill Grove, the farm was on Perkiomen Creek near Philadelphia. Fisher, he knew, could be trusted to take care of his son while the boy was learning about the operation of the farm.

When young Audubon reached the vicinity of Philadelphia, his father's friend saw to it that he was comfortably installed in a boardinghouse in nearby Norristown. This did not suit Audubon. Without asking anyone's advice or permission he moved over to Mill Grove Farm, where he thought he would prefer to live. Once at the farm he settled in with the tenants, a Quaker family named Thomas, and found great happiness. "Mill Grove," he said, "was a blessed place to me. There, with music, with hunting, riding beautiful horses and visiting congenial spirits, I was happy as happy could be."

Gregarious as Jean-Jacques was, he soon made the acquaintance of the young people of the neighborhood, who invited him to join them in their gatherings and excursions. But best of all, from his own point of view, he could wander at will through the nearby woods and fish the streams. He shot and drew birds and animals as he had never been able to do in France. In time he met on the neighboring farm of Fatland Ford an attractive English girl named Lucy Bakewell. He had avoided her house at first because of his prejudice against the English, but a chance encounter with her father led him to return his call. The result was exciting. As he himself tells it, he fell in love with Lucy at first sight.

The chief drawback to life at Mill Grove was young Audubon's unsatisfactory relationship with his father's overseer, a hard-nosed Frenchman named Dacosta, for whom, as for many persons who were to know Audubon, the young man's hunting and painting were mere trifling and a sign of reluctance to do serious work. Dacosta was persuaded that the small lead deposits found on the farm might be worked to advantage. Young Audubon was supposed to help in this enterprise, but the truth was that he thought the whole business a bore, and his indifference led Dacosta to think him an idler. Surprisingly,

3

however, he once told Audubon that he might have a future as a naturalist, and this praise, coming from so unlikely a source, pleased the young man greatly. He knew that in the main Dacosta's opinion of him was unfavorable.

Indeed the overseer remained staunch in his bad opinion of the boy's character, and he made the fact known with great frequency in letters to his employer. We may speculate, on the basis of his conduct, that the critical overseer was secretly pleased to see his employer's son turning out badly, for he nourished an ill-concealed desire to become the sole owner of the property he was supposed to be managing. Thus Dacosta, as shareholder and later as half owner of the property, found that the presence of a fractious and unambitious heir suited him admirably. On one occasion, after a particularly bitter disagreement with young Audubon, he tried to have him shanghaied to China, but Jean-Jacques succeeded in breaking away and made his way to France, where he protested violently to his father of Dacosta's treacherous action.

As far as one can tell, Lieutenant Audubon listened patiently to his son's angry complaints against Dacosta; but he seemed to have had an unwarranted confidence in the man and agreed with him that some strictures against his son's hunting, shooting, and sketching were justified. He had been urging Dacosta to be patient with the boy and to teach him how to work diligently. Now Jean-Jacques, seemingly as undisciplined as ever, stood before him, and Lieutenant Audubon decided at this point that his son needed closer supervision than Dacosta could provide. In his view he needed a companion and mentor, and for the purpose he chose Ferdinand Rozier. This young man, who was eight years older than Jean-Jacques, had a reputation for steadiness and business acumen. Furthermore he was eager to settle in the New World and make his fortune there. Jean-Jacques was accordingly sent back to Mill Grove in Rozier's company.

4

To this he made no objection. He and Rozier were on easy terms with each other.

On May 28, 1806, the two of them landed in New York and made their way to the place of business of William Bakewell, an uncle of Lucy Bakewell, whom Audubon had already decided to marry. There, before journeying on to Mill Grove, they announced their partnership. From this time forth Audubon was to anglicize his name and call himself John James Audubon. He had been warned by his father that it might be politic to conceal the fact of his illegitimacy in his new country, and he did so. It was perhaps because he hid the secret of his birth so well that many persons who studied his life reached interesting but totally erroneous conclusions concerning his origin.

# 2

# TO THE WOODS OF KENTUCKY

O<small>N</small> A<small>UGUST</small> 31, 1807, John James Audubon and Ferdinand Rozier left Mill Grove Farm for the town of Louisville, where they proposed to establish a general store. Their stock-in-trade, to be furnished them on credit by Benjamin Bakewell, was to be shipped to its destination in the usual fashion—by wagon to Pittsburgh and thence by flatboat down the Ohio River to Louisville.

Neither of the partners had ever been in truly wild country before, whether in Kentucky or elsewhere, but though the prospect may have daunted Rozier somewhat, it held no terrors for Audubon. Within miles of Perkiomen Creek he had come to know every thicket and stream, and the wild creatures that he had hunted and drawn represented most of the species of birds and animals to be found within a two or three days' hike of Mill Grove Farm. The phoebe, which he drew in a cave near the river in the year 1804, was but the first of the American birds that were to become his lifetime study. His drawing of the wood thrush dates from 1806. But not all of Audubon's accomplishments were those of art and of the out of doors: he had learned to play the flute and the violin well, he could dance beautifully, and he could handle a blade with the best of the swordsmen.

In one most important sense the thought of leaving Philadelphia and its environs for a new country was not a cheerful one for Audubon. Each mile he traveled westward through Pennsylvania in the jolting stagecoach was taking him farther away from his beloved Lucy. But there was consolation to be derived from the journey. Only if he proved himself a merchant capable of earning his living through his own efforts would Lucy's cautious father and his own father consent to their marriage. Thus in a sense every step away from Lucy now was ultimately a step toward her.

During the preceding year he had had the feeling that he was buried alive in Benjamin Bakewell's counting house in New York, while the more fortunate Rozier was serving his commercial apprenticeship in a similar business house in Philadelphia. As the months passed, Audubon could not convince himself that his boring work was profiting him very much, and he was pleased to learn that Rozier was becoming equally restless among the ledgers. Both young men were beginning to feel, in spite of their ignorance and inexperience, that if they were going to start a store on the frontier, there was no time like the present to begin.

True, Rozier knew very little about this vast new country; he had been here for little more than fourteen months, and he could speak English only with the greatest difficulty. But Audubon, almost an American after his several years of residence, was more knowledgeable. He had listened to the stories of travelers about the sparsely settled country beyond the Allegheny Mountains. In particular he had heard enthusiastic reports of the small settlement of Louisville, a sort of rendezvous for trappers and traders situated on the Ohio far down the river from Pittsburgh, and he persuaded Rozier that they would do well to begin their venture there. Accordingly the partners made arrangements to procure capital by signing a note to Benjamin Bakewell for a stock-in-trade which they directed to be forwarded to them in Louisville. No one in the family, apparently, put any obstacles in their way or suggested that their action was premature.

As the westward journey began, Rozier had little more than a marginal interest in the wild and beautiful country through which they were passing. Then, as later, his eyes were on the main chance. Wilderness travel and exotic scenery were incidental, even boring to him. What he wanted above all was to reach his destination, to set up a store, and to start making money. Still it was he, rather than the more sensitive Audubon, who has left us the only full account of their journey that we have. Audubon, we may suppose, was too busy with his observations of nature to think of keeping a diary. He had managed to find the time for sketching, hunting, and taxidermy even while he was supposedly devoting himself full time to learning the methods of business in New York City. His drawing of the spring tail duck is dated August 22, 1807, a convincing proof that his interest in birds had waned not at all during his apprenticeship. Now that he was finally on the road west we may be sure that he was eternally busy with hunting and drawing.

Rozier's account of their journey, though lacking in the imaginative touches that his partner would have provided instinctively, is still as fresh as the day it was written. A translation reads:

On the thirty-first day of August, 1807, in company with Audubon, I left Mill Grove for Louisville, Kentucky, where we anticipated engaging in the mercantile business.

Leaving Philadelphia by stage we traveled to Lancaster, Pennsylvania, a distance of sixty-one miles, where we arrived at four o'clock in the afternoon; we dined, and proceeded to Big Chickers, distant nine miles farther, where we spent the night. The roads from Philadelphia to Lancaster were in excellent condition, and at about every two miles we found good taverns. The only remarkable thing we noticed in agriculture was hemp, there being little else of interest. The city of Lancaster was attractive, but the short duration of our stay prevented us from having more than a casual view of it. The tavern where we slept

8

was not very good; from our chambers, however, we could discern a new bridge, which had two immense arches spanning the river.

At eight o'clock in the morning we left Lancaster for Elizabethtown, distant nine miles. The roads were miserable, and we suffered a severe jolting and shaking up. Arriving there, we procured two additional horses, which made six all told, and went on to Middletown, where we breakfasted at a tavern named the "Eagle"; the village was small, with few houses, and nothing of interest. . . .

The remainder of our journey was by way of the Ohio, and we made it entirely in an open flatboat, a cumbersome, unwieldy craft, managed by hand, and in this particular instance very badly. One who has never had this experience can little understand the terrible monotony, hardships and deprivations encountered on a long journey such as we endured. We were unprotected from the elements, and our beds consisted of bare pine boards, upon which we slept as best we could, enveloped in our great coats.

There were times without number when our boat would run upon hidden sand bars to become grounded, and we were then obliged to get into the cold water and assist in the work of extricating her. At other times, unprotected as we were the rains drenched us to the skin, and our clothing was so saturated that it took many hours to dry. At night when it was clear, we continued our course down the river, but, in bad weather, or when very cloudy and dark, we were obliged to tie up to the shore, frequently to the bank of some wild, uninhabited island, and wait there for daylight; then we would resume our slow, tedious, and seemingly never ending journey. Added to these hardships, our boat was commanded by a most disagreeable and ungentlemanly captain, named Harris; his language and demeanor marked him as a person of low birth and bad character. . . .

Audubon's description of the river portion of a western journey dates from a slightly later period, but the circumstances of this trip cannot have been much different from those of his first. I append it here as a contrast to Rozier's account, particularly in view of Audubon's more poetic

9

treatment of what to Rozier was undoubtedly a prosaic experience:

As night came, sinking into darkness the broader portions of the river, our minds became affected by strong emotions, and wandered far beyond the present moments. The tinkling of bells told us that the cattle which bore them were gently roving from valley to valley in search of food, or returning to their distant homes. The hooting of the Great Owl, or the muffled noise of its wings as it sailed smoothly over the stream, were matters of interest to us; so was the sound of the boatman's horn, as it came winding more and more softly from afar. When daylight returned, many songsters burst forth with echoing notes, more and more mellow to the listening ear. Here and there the lonely cabin of a squatter struck the eye, giving note of commencing civilization. The crossing of the stream by a deer foretold how soon the hills would be covered by snow.

Many sluggish flatboats we overtook and passed; some laden with produce from the different head-waters of the small rivers that pour their tributary streams into the Ohio; others, of less dimensions, crowded with immigrants from distant parts, in search of a new home.

The margins of the shores and of the river were at this season amply supplied with game. A Wild Turkey, a Grouse, or a Blue-winged Teal, could be procured in a few moments; and we fared well, for, whenever we pleased, we landed, struck up a fire and provided, as we were, with the necessary utensils, procured a good repast.

The reader notices at once with amusement that in his first account of river travel and its trials Rozier displays a city man's instinctive dislike for such painful chores as getting down into the ice cold water to help pull the boat off the sand bars. Audubon, on the other hand, though actually little more experienced in wilderness living than his partner, found his new adventures stimulating. One remembers that once while ice-skating on Perkiomen Creek with Lucy Bakewell and other young people, he had fallen through the surface and had imperturbably managed to float along underwater to another opening in the thick ice, where he bobbed up, remaining quite unfrightened by the almost fatal accident. Audubon was, in a word, a born outdoorsman. He absorbed lessons in woodcraft from his surroundings as readily as Daniel Boone, whom he came to know and admire. From the outset the woods were his element as surely as the counting house and retail store were Rozier's. For Audubon the rain, the wettings, the sleet, the cold, the snow—in short, all the discomforts of the trail—were to be taken in stride, enjoyed, and, frequently, laughed at.

# 3

# LOUISVILLE, 1807

DESCRIPTIONS OF EARLY Louisville abound. They come from the pens of many observers and vary only in detail. All agree that the village of 1807 numbered some 1,300 souls. One writer described the town thus: "It consisted of one principal and handsome street, about half a mile long, tolerably compactly built, and the houses generally superior, many of three stories, with a parapet wall on top, which in front gives the appearance of having flat roofs." In all directions except toward the river the settlement was surrounded by deep woods. Its situation on a promontory, overlooking a bend in the river, was ideal for the trading post it already was and for the city it was to become. The hills on the Indiana shore had been dubbed the Silver Hills, but they reminded many a beholder of the green slopes of Switzerland. The wild river was far prettier than the tame river of today, for it was as yet unmarred by evidences of man's selfishness and his disregard for nature. As far as one could see, the banks were lined with majestic forests, the only pollution the occasional smoke from the chimneys of the town or the campfire of an Indian or trapper in the woods. The stream was still, in short, what La Salle had called it, *La Belle Rivière*.

For the weary Rozier and the enthusiastic Audubon, the sight of the little town around the bend, small and unpretentious though it was, spelled the end of a long journey. We have no first-hand account from either partner of their first days in Louisville. After they had stepped ashore from their boat, one supposes that Audubon would have been content to find a sheltered place to lay his bed roll, while Rozier's more urban tastes demanded a room in a hotel.

The only such accommodation available, the Indian Queen, was run by the amiable and influential John Gwathmey and his wife. These good people, along with Mrs. Gwathmey's brothers the Clarks, soon became close friends of Audubon. They seem to have been popular with their guests, and we know that they had status with the people of the town—which is to say that the Gwathmeys must have run a clean and honest establishment and, above all, that they had managed to find a good cook. After all, good cooks were harder to come by than good food in a spot so remote from city comforts. Wild game was easy to procure: if a man wanted meat for his dinner, it sufficed for him to stroll into the woods a few hundred yards from the hostelry to bring down game or birds in plenty. But cooking the meat properly was something else again, and the chef of the Indian Queen seems to have known his trade. Evidently he was not of the "burn it or leave it raw" school that often passed for cooking on the frontier, as widely among whites as among Indians; and the two new settlers were lucky to sit at his table.

It has been argued that during their first days in Louisville Audubon and Rozier did not actually open a store but followed paths in the woods, carrying heavy packs stuffed to the brim with goods such as needles, thread, yard goods, cornmeal, coffee, tea, and whiskey—to satisfy the needs of pioneers living in small settlements or isolated cabins not too far from Louisville. It seems probable that they did attempt to dispose of some of their goods in this fashion, but it must also be true that they set up a central depository or store in town where they could keep their stocks, and where they could attract buyers from the town of Louisville itself.

It did not take the partners long to find out that business could as readily result in loss as in gain. One of their first orders was lost completely. This led Audubon, who remembered his failures in business more readily than his successes, to remark later in life: "The mercantile business did not suit me. The very first venture I undertook was in indigo . . . the whole of which was lost."

Soon the partners, or at least the junior partner, began to make friends in the new town. Audubon was not the sort of man who needed much time to get acquainted. In whatever company he found himself, whether in drawing room, tavern, or hunter's cabin in the woods, he developed new friendships rapidly. He was quick to discover, for instance, that about five miles downstream from Louisville at the Falls of the Ohio there lived some score of well-to-do Frenchmen in a settlement called Shippingport. Audubon was never clannish to the point of seeking out the company of Frenchmen merely on the basis of their nationality and language, but among the Shippingport folk he found a number of persons with whom he had much in common. These French refugees made a good living on the frontier, but besides being good businessmen they were cultivated people in the European manner. They enjoyed many of the same things that Audubon did—music, dancing, hunting, and even nature study of a serious sort.

Of all the French families among whom Audubon found special friends, two stand out: the Tarascons, from Marseilles, and the Berthouds. In their own country several of the families had pretensions to nobility, but in the United States they lived as members of the middle class. Audubon found special links with both families. Jean and Louis Tarascon, who were millers, were acquainted with Audubon's friends the Bakewells, while the Berthouds were to become not only lifelong friends, but, through the marriage of Nicholas Berthoud to Lucy Bakewell's sister, relatives as well. Both of the Berthouds—James, the elder, and Nicholas, the younger—did many a service for Audubon. In later years, when fame began to knock at his door, the younger Berthoud became the business manager for the *Birds of America.*

There were many other friends too, such as the Irishman Major William Croghan, an influential businessman of the town and a veteran of the Revolutionary War. Croghan was allied through his wife with the Clark family, two of whose members Audubon was to know intimately. George Rogers Clark, the Revolutionary War general and hero, was now partially paralyzed but still active mentally. He was considered the founder of Louisville and lived near town at Locust Grove. His younger brother, William, had just returned home in triumph from his celebrated expedition to the Oregon country in the company of Captain Meriwether Lewis. Croghan and the two Clarks took a liking to Audubon at once. Croghan was particularly interested in him since he had been acquainted with his father during the war with Britain. William Clark, the explorer, shared with Audubon a common interest in sketching. As part of his report to President Jefferson concerning the western expedition of 1803–1806, he had done a number of sketches of noteworthy birds, animals, and places observed during the long cross-country journey. He was not a practiced artist, but in his sketches he succeeded in conveying a realistic image of what he had seen. One imagines the pleasure Audubon took in studying his scientific notebooks. Nearby in Louisville itself lived the famous Dr. William C. Galt, a passionate amateur naturalist, who at once recognized in Audubon a talented fellow amateur and was delighted to hear him confess that during his days of business apprenticeship in New York, when he was supposed to be concentrating his attention entirely on business concerns, he had spent his evenings doing taxidermy for another well-known naturalist, Samuel Latham Mitchill, a friend of Galt's and later a founding father of the New York Lyceum of Natural History.

It was in fact during these early days in Louisville, when once again he was supposed to be fully occupied, when Rozier expected him to bend every nerve in the development of their new business, that Audubon did some of the best studies of birds that he achieved in Kentucky. To this period we owe his sketches of the orchard oriole (1808), the kingfisher and whippoorwill (1810), and the Carolina parrakeet (1811). One year later he drew the nighthawk. Thus did Audubon's drawing of birds go on without interruption at a time when he had no clue about what he would ultimately do with his accumulation. Nor did he regard any of his completed drawings as definitive. He was constantly revising his work, for he was generally dissatisfied with it. He thought nothing of spending hours redrawing and repainting his earlier sketches, and of consigning the originals to the fire.

Rozier, meanwhile, had no such time-consuming and soul-satisfying hobby to claim his attention and take his mind off his work. He did not benefit from the host of new and delightfully interlocking friendships that so filled Audubon's days. He was totally lacking in the variety and complexity of outside interests that made his partner such a welcome visitor in the drawing room, nor had he, apparently, the useful gift of small talk. Thus where Audubon was pleased to spend countless hours roaming the forest trails with hunting companions or lounging idly before the fireplaces of his newfound friends, believing optimistically that every new contact was a gain for business (or perhaps not giving a thought to business at all), the elder partner was busy in the shop all day. Audubon meanwhile was nowhere to be seen.

It must be said in all fairness that Rozier was not without a reason for his worries. When the partners had begun their enterprise, the firm of Benjamin Bakewell had lent them the sum of $3647.29; and the prospect of repaying the loan within the specified time limit of eight months had to be calculated carefully. Besides, there was trouble brewing in the nation's economy, and it all came to a head just three days before Christmas, when the Congress passed the Embargo Act forbidding American vessels to sail for foreign ports. This attempt to keep America out of a European war was a boon to national security, but in the narrower view of some of the merchants who were dependent for their profits on foreign trade, the decision was a disastrous one, driving many a firm, including that of Benjamin Bakewell, out of business.

The bad news spread fairly soon to the Kentucky frontier, and its implications touched Audubon where they could hurt him most, that is, by casting a cloud over his marriage prospects. Did he dare, despite the evidence of business stagnation everywhere, to go ahead with his marriage plans? Above all, would his prospective father-in-law agree to such a step? Sober questions, but to one of Audubon's sunny disposition their answers could only be in the affirmative. To settle the matter he would go east in the spring and try to persuade William Bakewell that despite all evidence to the contrary the prospects for business in Louisville were good. To win a favorable decision would probably require some fast talking, but where Lucy was concerned, Audubon was sure of his powers of persuasion. Happily the two partners were ready to make good on their note, due April 9. This achievement would surely be a talking point in Audubon's favor.

If at this same time Audubon gave any thought to the problem of keeping a city-bred girl happy on the frontier, he has said nothing about it; but he must have counted heavily on his friends. As he expected them to help him in his business, he also thought of their wives as potential friends and companions of Lucy. Thus her sacrifice in leaving the social world of suburban Philadelphia would be far less painful for her than otherwise. In Shippingport she would be assured of a warm welcome. It was with a certain optimism, therefore, that Audubon prepared for his trip east.

When the time came, the partners left Louisville together. It is difficult to imagine how Audubon and Rozier could have persuaded themselves that they could both leave their business at the same time, but leave it they did to make their way east by the usual route. In March they closed up their shop and headed for Fatland Ford. To the prospective bridegroom the country had never looked more attractive. Spring was coming to Pennsylvania as it was to Kentucky, and Lucy, when he saw her, looked prettier than ever.

The meeting of the lovers was tender, and, happily, there seem to have been no serious objections raised to their imminent wedding by the father of the bride. The situation had changed radically in the Bakewell home during the intervening year. Some time after the death of Lucy's mother, which occurred before Audubon left for Kentucky, William Bakewell had remarried. His new wife was Rebecca Smith, a stiff-necked and disagreeable woman with whom Lucy found herself on bad terms. Her wishes had been openly expressed: she would spend no more time than was absolutely necessary under the same roof with her stepmother. The new Mrs. Bakewell seems to have disliked Audubon almost before she had seen him, and poor William Bakewell, who did like him, realized the need for peace in his household. What was more natural, then, than to give the young people his blessing without more ado. Apparently the formerly reluctant Lieutenant Audubon gave his consent also. Plans for the wedding went forward as rapidly as possible.

In the few days remaining before the date of the wedding, the engaged couple spent their leisure time wandering about in their favorite woods and rural haunts. Audubon painted birds and studied their habits as he used to do. A phoebe to whose leg he had attached a silver thread two years earlier ("loose enough," he said, "not to hurt the part, yet so fastened that no exertion of theirs could remove it") came back with the thread still in place. Audubon was pleased to see him, but seems to have attached no special significance to this wonderful occurrence, which has become celebrated as the first example of bird banding in the United States.

# 4

# THE STOREKEEPER
# TAKES A WIFE

THE WEDDING DAY of John James Audubon and Lucy Bakewell finally dawned. Not a pleasant day, it was foggy and windy. The ceremony took place on April 5, 1808, and was performed by the Reverend Mr. William Latta, minister of two nearby Chester County Presbyterian churches. The following announcement of the wedding appeared in the *Norristown Weekly Register:* "Married on Tues. the 5th inst., by the Rev. William Latta, Mr. J. Audubon of Louisville, to Miss Lucy Bakewell, eldest daughter of Mr. Bakewell, of Fatland Ford, in this county."

Audubon's description of himself at about this time, composed later, gives us a good picture of the man Lucy Bakewell married. He said of himself: "I measured five feet ten and one half inches, was of fair mien, and quite a handsome figure: large, dark and rather sunken eyes, light colored eyebrows, aquiline nose and a fine set of teeth; hair fine textured and luxuriant, divided and passing down behind each ear in luxuriant ringlets as far as the shoulders."

This pen portrait, if a bit self-satisfied, was also candid. Long hair of the sort Audubon described himself as wearing was not in style at the time; yet no protest on the part of his friends (and they did protest from time to time) succeeded in making him a regular patron of the barber.

As for Lucy, most observers agree that although her features did not entitle her to be called beautiful, she was decidedly attractive, and many thought her pretty.

In the next few days preparation for the westward journey of the young couple kept the Bakewell house astir. Then finally they were off. For Audubon it was a return to a part of the country he already knew, but for Lucy it was a high and somewhat fearsome adventure. Audubon has left us no description of the trip, but except for the joyous fact of its being a honeymoon the actual travel must have resembled in most particulars the identical journey of the two partners during the preceding summer. Rozier, as we know, was with Audubon this time also. For Lucy alone the views and occurrences of the trip held the excitement of the completely unknown and she it is who will tell us about it.

Generally their trip was uneventful. There was but one untoward incident to report. During the passage of one of the all-but-impossible roads over the Allegheny Mountains, the stagecoach overturned with several passengers inside, including a frightened Lucy Audubon. Her husband was not sitting beside her in the coach, for he was among the men who had volunteered to get out and walk alongside to lighten the load. In fact he was fond of walking ahead of the coach in any case, for he was thus enabled to observe the wildlife that fled before the stage. After the accident it was discovered on examination that Lucy had broken no bones, but she was badly shaken up, and she admitted that the occurrence heightened her already notable distaste for travel. It was also a frightening experience for her anxious husband.

The thoughts that passed through Lucy Audubon's mind both before and after her accident cannot have been altogether confident. As the favorite daughter of an indulgent and fairly well-to-do father, she was used to being supplied with every comfort. Now with each turn of the wheels she was facing a change from the easy, civilized life of suburban Philadelphia to a life of the frontier, and the full implications of this awesome prospect may well have given her an occasional twinge of terror. The Louisville of 1808 was hardly a sophisticated place, and in Lucy's anticipation it must have been imagined as even wilder and woolier than it actually was. But Lucy loved her John James dearly and had loved him for several years. Her decision to marry him and follow his fortunes west was unshakable. The corrosive effect of her stepmother's personality merely served to increase her determination to marry and set up her own home, as far as possible from the sound of Rebecca Bakewell's voice.

When Rozier and the Audubons finally stepped ashore at Louisville after their long coach ride, followed in its turn by nine days on the river, Lucy was understandably tired. They went at once to their lodgings in the Indian Queen and retired. Although they had no inkling of it at the time, they were to make the hotel their home for more than two years. On the day of arrival, common ablutions at the pump in the courtyard of the inn and the necessity of passing through other people's sleeping quarters in order to reach her own were shocks to Lucy's city-bred expectations, but their own room was comfortable and she and her husband soon grew used to hotel life. Three copious meals were served each day in a large but crowded dining room. It was here in the Indian Queen that their first son, Victor Gifford Audubon, was born on June 12, 1809, some thirteen months after their arrival in Louisville.

Audubon was quick to introduce his wife to all the friends he had made in the town and in nearby Shippingport during his bachelor year, and like him Lucy was quick to form new attachments. In a short while she had a full circle of friends among the Clarks, the Berthouds, the Tarascons and the Croghans. This gift of friendship was to be one of Lucy's greatest assets, for in the years to come, the closer her husband came to fame, the more often he was to leave his wife and children in the hands of his friends while he traveled about the country in the pursuit of wild birds. As Lucy once put it, "I have a rival in every bird."

Evidently Lucy's scant knowledge of French was no handicap in the midst of her new acquaintances. She had already begun to take a few lessons in the language before leaving Philadelphia, and she ultimately became proficient enough to give lessons herself. Besides, the French refugees on the American frontier were not the sort to brood about the eroding of their French heritage. They had expected something of the sort to happen. All of them, however they felt about the French Revolution and its Napoleonic aftermath, had decided to cast their lot permanently in the New World among English speakers. They kept abreast of events in the old country, and their business dealings included transactions with French firms. As bilinguals, when they needed to use French for social or commercial reasons they could do so without hesitation. The rest of the time they felt no self-consciousness, even among themselves, about expressing their ideas in such English as they could muster. The same was true of Audubon, whose English, like that of his compatriots, kept improving with use. As a proof of his growing proficiency there is the fact that he was already writing to his father in English.

Shortly after her arrival in Louisville Lucy wrote a letter to her cousin, Euphemia Gifford, in Derby, England. This letter has often been quoted, but mostly in patchwork fashion. As it appears below it is complete except for two short passages irrelevant to the matters at hand:

*Louisville, Kentucky*
*May 27, 1808*

*My dear Cousin,*
*My papa has, I imagine, before this time informed you of my change of situation. My marriage took place in the beginning of April. I soon afterwards left home and entered on my new*

duties. As yet they have been light, and be they what they may I hope I shall ever cheerfully perform them. I wish you were acquainted with the partner of my destiny. It is useless to say more of him to you at so great a distance, than that he has most excellent dispositions which add very much to the happiness of my married life. I wish, my dear Cousin, you could have enjoyed the variety [of] beautiful prospects we did on our journey without partaking of the fatigues. However, considering the length of it I must not complain. We traveled something more than three hundred miles by land and seven hundred by water. You will form some idea of the roads when I tell you that the first day we travel[ed] seventy miles, set out at four in the morning and arrived at the end at about seven in the evening, and every day afterwards, traveling the same number of hours we could only go between thirty and forty. Unfortunately we had rain most of the way or I intended to walk a great deal for whilst the stage is going either up or down the mountains they move as slowly forwards as possible, but great stones beneath the wheels make the stage rock about most dreadfully. After the two first days we commenced climbing the mountains. We crossed the low mountains, the Allegheny, the Laurel, the Sidling and many others which are very stony and disagreeable to pass through. They are not mentioned in the maps. The Cove Mount is the highest, I think, that we passed and also the most stony, although there is great deal more said of the Allegheny mountain. We staid at Pittsburgh two weeks. It is situated at the extremity of Pennsylvania just at the junction of three rivers, the Allegheny, [Monongahela,] and Ohio. High mountains on all sides environ Pittsburgh, and a thick fog is almost constant over the town. . . . The seven hundred miles by water was performed without much fatigue though not without some disagreeables. Our conveyance was a large, square or rather oblong boat, but perfectly flat on all sides; and just high enough to admit a person walking upright. There are no sails made use of owing to the many turns in the river which brings the wind from every quarter in the course of an hour or two. The boat is carried along by the current, and in general without the least motion, but one day we had so high a wind as to make some of us feel a little sea sick. Bread, beer and ham we bought at Pittsburgh, but poultry, eggs and milk can always be bought from the farm houses on the banks. There are not many exten-

24

*sive prospects on the river as the shores are in general bounded by high rocks covered with wood[s]. However, I was gratified by the sight of a great variety of foliage and flowers. There are many small towns on the way some of which we stopped at. Mr. Audubon regretted he had not his drawing implements with him as he would have taken some views for you. However, there are some well worth taking in this neighbourhood when he has got a little more settled and has arranged his business. We traveled generally at night, and reached the place of our future residence, which [is] a very pleasantly situated place; the country around is rather flat, but the land is very fertile. I cannot quite tell how I shall like Louisville as I have only been here three weeks and have not yet got a house; but I have received every attention from the inhabitants. . . . Where we board we have very accommo[dating] people. . . . we are as private as we please. . . . Most of the houses here have gardens adjoining, and some of them are very prettily laid out indeed. Vegetation is a month or six weeks forwarder here than in Pennsylvania or York State. I am very sorry there is no Library here or book store of any kind for I have very few of my own and as Mr. Audubon is constantly at the store I should often enjoy a book very much whilst I am alone. I hope, my dear Cousin, your health is quite established. . . . My husband unites with myself in affectionate regards to yourself from whom I hope I shall hear soon. Believe me*

> *My Dear Cousin*
> *Yours ever affectionately*
> *L. Audubon*

Lucy might also have added, had she cared to do so, that the city already had a courthouse, a theater, and a market, and that a third newspaper was just beginning to be published.

Audubon's own comment on his progress as a Louisville merchant, to be found in his story of his life, is unexpectedly brief and to the point. Of their new enterprise he says: "We had many goods and opened up a large store in Louisville which went on prospering, when I attended to it." The pertinent phrase in the sentence is, of course, the revealing one "when I attended to it," for as we have seen, the devoted Rozier carried on alone most of the burdens of the partnership. Audubon, naturally, had his share of things to do, and neither at this time nor at any other could he have been called lazy or a wilfull shirker, but to Rozier, who was utterly devoted to the business, the division of labor between him and his junior partner must have seemed at times no division at all. Too often Audubon went hunting in the woods, sketched in his room, or visited with friends by the hour—while Rozier waited on trade or wrestled with the inventories.

The diligent storekeeper was rapidly revealing himself a competent merchant, as a glance at the books will show. By December 1808 the firm had sent to Benjamin Bakewell nearly $3,000 of the $4,804 owed for new goods. Audubon's comment on their standing is a trifle sardonic. He was to write later in *The Story of My Life:* "Birds were birds, then as now, and my thoughts were ever and anon turning towards them as objects of my greatest delight. I shot, I drew, I looked on nature only; my days were happy beyond human conception, and beyond that I really cared not. . . . I seldom passed a day without drawing a bird, or noting something respecting its habits. Rozier meantime attended the counter. I could relate many curious anecdotes about him, but never mind them: he made out to grow rich, and what more could he ask for?"

Among the most famous of the birds that Audubon sketched in those early days was the spectacular cardinal grosbeak, done in watercolors and presented to his friend Dr. William Galt, who, as we have noted, shared his interest in wildlife and ornithology. This gift was a characteristic gesture; for though the artist cherished his growing stock of bird portraits, he could not resist the temptation to give one away occasionally as a present to someone whose friendship he valued.

One of Audubon's most constant companions in his wanderings through the woods in search of birds was the store's young clerk, Nathaniel Pope, whom he and Rozier had hired to help attend to the trade. Together Audubon and Pope spent many an hour rambling in the wilds. To Rozier such conduct must have seemed like adding insult to injury. But despite the disparity of temperament between the partners, there is no evidence that they ever quarreled or that they came close to doing so. If Rozier complained, it was without bitterness, and also quite without persuading the younger man to change his ways. Rozier had the patience of Job, and Audubon the nonchalance of genius. There really was not enough work to keep two men and a clerk busy; still for the record, there is Audubon's consistent failure to take his duties seriously.

Just before Christmas the following year Audubon went east to buy more trading goods for the store. Most of these trips, like this one of December 1809, were successful both as business ventures and as ornithological expeditions, especially the latter. Audubon could not refrain from sketching birds. He also liked to ride horseback, and many of his trips were made in this way. He knew the horse for a quicker and more enjoyable means of transportation than the keelboat, especially eastbound, against the current. If during the western part of the journey he tired of riding, he could always load his horse on a flatboat and continue by river. On all occasions when traveling alone he preferred the horse to the stagecoach on the stretch of road between Pittsburgh and Philadelphia. He admits with but scant apology that on these trips he often indulged his interest in birds at the expense of his commercial mission. He himself tells how on one trip he grew so intrigued by some warblers that while pursuing them he entirely forgot the existence of the pack animals he had with him, and when he went back to look for them they had disappeared without a trace. Nor was this the only example of his absentmindedness. Once in the Kentucky woods he allowed a horse whose saddlebags contained a sizable sum of money to wander from his sight, but on this occasion luck was with him, and he recovered both his horse and his money.

From Audubon's narratives of life around him as he observed it, we see that he and his wife were spectators and participants in the festivals that came with the seasons. Here is Audubon's description of a Fourth of July celebration on the frontier:

Each pretty lass, in pure white, rode with her sturdy lover on a steed whose neighing proclaimed how proud the creature was of its burden. Each couple leaped down, and after twisting the bridle around a branch, they joined the barbecue. Soon the grounds were alive with humanity. A great wooden cannon bound with hoops and crammed with homemade powder boomed a salute amid hearty huzzas. A good oration from the most learned gladdened every ear. Although it did not equal the eloquence of a Henry Clay, an Edward Everett or a Daniel Webster or some others of note, it nevertheless reminded every Kentuckian present of the glorious name, patriotism, courage, and virtue of our immortal George Washington. Fifes and drums sounded the march. The strains of "Yankee Doodle" brought an uproar.

In this same account Audubon mentions that those of the men who refrained from dancing amused themselves by driving nails with a rifle bullet or barking squirrels. This latter sport, said to have been demonstrated to Audubon by Daniel Boone, consisted of aiming just close enough to a squirrel's perch to cause his death from concussion. An eyewitness also informs us that Audubon, who was no more a stranger to dancing than he was to marksmanship, on occasion led some of the dances with his violin and showed himself a most enthusiastic caller.

Audubon's description of the Fourth of July celebration is but one of many prose tales with which he interlarded his work. He presents a fairly comprehensive picture of life in Kentucky in the days when he first lived there in those descriptions of maple sugar-making, coon hunts, wolf baiting, a tornado (referred to by him as a hurricane), and other colorful events.

# 5

# A MEMORABLE
# MEETING

By 1810 AUDUBON'S portfolios were bulging with more than two hundred bird portraits. He was no longer a novice painter, and he knew his own skill. In March of that year his famous meeting with Alexander Wilson took place. This Scottish ornithologist, who preceded him in the systematic study of American birds, was traveling about the country seeking new species. But as his publication was far advanced, he was also anxious to obtain subscriptions for his book.

The encounter of the two naturalists was a historic occasion from every point of view. Accounts of the meeting conflict in many ways, and it is all but impossible to tell where the truth lies. Did the two artists meet cordially and as friends? The principals themselves disagree. Unfortunately for Audubon's reputation, the relevant passages in Wilson's diary were edited and published three years after the event by George Ord, a Philadelphia naturalist and close friend of Wilson's. Ord had the academician's contempt for the self-taught, and because he expected to derive a reputation from his sponsorship of Wilson's work, he was even more jealous than the Scotsman of the upstart Kentuckian who might rival his friend and protégé. Consequently Ord bore Audubon an almost fanatical ill will. Here are the cogent passages from Wilson's journal as edited and published by Ord:

March 17. Take my baggage and grope my way to Louisville—put up at the Indian Queen tavern, and gladly sit down to rest myself.

March 18. Rise quite refreshed. Find a number of land speculators here.

March 19. Rambling round the town with my gun. Examined Mr. ——'s drawings in crayon—very good. Saw two new birds he had, both Motacillae.

March 20. Set out this afternoon with the gun—killed nothing new (People in taverns here devour their meals. many shopkeepers board in taverns—also boatmen, land speculators, merchants &c.) *No naturalist to keep me company.*

March 21. Went out shooting this afternoon with Mr. A. Saw a number of Sandhill Cranes. Pigeons numerous.

March 22.

March 23. Packed up my things which I left in the care of a merchant here, to be sent on to Lexington; and having parted with great regret, with my paroquet, to the gentleman of the tavern, I bade adieu to Louisville, to which place I had four letters of recommendation, and was taught to expect much of everything there, but neither received one act of civility from those to whom I was recommended, one subscriber, *nor one new bird;* though I delivered my letters, ransacked the woods repeatedly, and visited all the characters likely to subscribe. *Science or literature* has *not one friend in this place. (Everyone is so intent on making money,* that they can talk of nothing else; and they absolutely devour their meals, that they may return sooner to their business. Their manners correspond with their features.)

This is harsh testimony on the town and its inhabitants. Taken by itself and at its face value, it also portrays Audubon in a poor light. He appears not only inhospitable to a fellow naturalist but downright indifferent as well. But over and against these remarks we must read and weigh Audubon's version of the same meeting. His episode entitled "Louisville in Kentucky" tells quite a different story:

One fair morning, I was surprised by the sudden entrance into our counting-room [at Louisville] of Mr. Alexander Wilson, the celebrated author of the "American Ornithology," of whose existence I had never until that moment been apprised. This happened in March, 1810. How well do I remember him, as he then walked up to me! His long, rather hooked nose, the keenness of his eyes, and his prominent cheek-bones, stamped his countenance with a peculiar character. His dress, too, was a kind not usually seen in that part of the country; a short coat, trousers, and a waistcoat of grey cloth. His stature was not above the middle size. He had two volumes under his arm, and as he approached the table at which I was working, I thought I discovered something like astonishment in his countenance. He, however, immediately proceeded to disclose the object of his visit, which was to procure subscriptions for his work. He opened his books, explained the nature of his occupations, and requested my patronage.

I felt surprised and gratified at the sight of the volumes, turned over a few of the plates, and had already taken a pen to write my name in his favour when my partner rather abruptly said to me in French, "My dear Audubon, what induces you to subscribe to this work? Your drawings are certainly far better, and again you must know as much of the habits of American birds as this gentleman." Whether Mr. Wilson understood French or not, or if the suddeness with which I paused, disappointed him, I cannot tell; but I clearly perceived that he was not pleased. Vanity and the encomiums of my friend prevented me from subscribing. Mr. Wilson asked me if I had many drawings of birds. I rose, took down a large portfolio, laid it on the table, and showed him, as I would show you, kind reader, or any other person fond of such subjects, the whole of the contents, with the same patience with which he had shown me his own engravings.

His surprise appeared great, as he told me he never had the most distant idea that any other individual than himself had been engaged in forming such a collection. He asked me if it was my intention to publish, and when I answered in the negative, his surprise seemed to increase. And, truly, such was not my intention; for, until long after, when I met the Prince of Musignano in Philadelphia, I had not the least idea of presenting the fruits of my labours to the world. Mr. Wilson now examined my drawings with care, asked if I should have any objections to lending him a few during his stay, to which I replied that I had none; he then bade me good morning, not, however, until I had made an arrangement to explore the woods in the vicinity along with him, and had promised to procure for him some birds, of which I had drawings in my collection, but which he had never seen.

It happened that he lodged in the same house with us, but his retired habits, I thought, exhibited either a strong feeling of discontent, or a decided melancholy. The Scotch airs which he played sweetly on his flute made me melancholy too, and I felt for him. I presented him to my wife and friends, and seeing that he was all enthusiasm, exerted myself as much as was in my power, to procure for him the specimens which he wanted. We hunted together, and obtained birds which he had never seen; but, reader, I did not subscribe to his work, for, even at that time, my collection was greater than his. Thinking that he might be pleased to publish the results of my researches, I offered them to him, merely on condition that what I had drawn, or might afterwards draw and send to him, should be mentioned in his work, as coming from my pencil. I at the same time offered to open a correspondence with him, which I thought might prove beneficial to us both. He made no reply to either proposal, and before many days had elapsed left Louisville, on his way to New Orleans, little knowing how much his talents were appreciated in our little town, at least by myself and my friends.

Some time elapsed, during which I never heard of him, or of his work. At length, having occasion to go to Philadelphia, I, immediately after my arrival there, inquired for him and paid him a visit. He was then drawing a White-headed Eagle. He received me with civility, and took me to the Exhibition Rooms of Rembrandt Peale, the artist, who had then portrayed Napoleon crossing the Alps. Mr. Wilson spoke not of birds or drawings. Feeling, as I was forced to do, that my company was not agreeable, I parted from him; and after that I never saw him again. But judge of my astonishment some time after, when on reading the thirty-ninth page of the ninth volume of American Ornithology, I found in it the following paragraph:

"March 23, 1810.—I bid adieu to Louisville, to which place I had four letters of recommendation, and was taught to expect much of everything there; but neither received one act of civility from those to whom I was recommended, one subscriber, nor one new bird. . . ."

We shall probably never know for sure what really happened between them, but it is fair to say this much: Wilson, who was throughout his life a much underrated and much put upon man, had acquired a somewhat crabbed and unamiable disposition, which he displayed to all comers. Audubon, who up to the time the two artists met had never known a serious setback of any kind, was open and generous to a fault. It would not have been in character for him to be uncivil to a fellow naturalist. It was his custom rather to welcome them all with open arms, as he describes himself as having done with Wilson. Furthermore there is the distinct possibility of George Ord's wilful tampering with the text. Before Wilson died, only seven volumes of his work had appeared, and the two posthumous volumes were practically written by Ord. He was to campaign for years to enhance Wilson's reputation and to discredit Audubon in every way he knew how. This being so, was the text of Wilson's diary sacred in his hands? Furthermore it cannot be totally irrelevant to the controversy that although the original manuscript of Wilson's journal was in Ord's possession as late as 1840, it disappeared after that date and has never since been found.

Despite the unfavorable view of Audubon that Ord and others found it possible to read into his encounter with Wilson, the meeting was, I believe, of seminal importance for Audubon. Up to this point the young naturalist-businessman had been driven to bird study by an inner compulsion that he himself did not understand. Incredible as it may seem, neither he nor his wife nor any of the friends who admired his sketches, with the possible exception of young Nathaniel Pope, seem to have regarded his paintings of American wild birds as anything more than a pleasant pastime. To some persons, and their number must have included his partner Rozier, bird painting was a hobby that Audubon unwisely allowed to interfere with more serious pursuits. In short, since aesthetic considerations were held to be inconsequential by the people of the frontier, his achievements as an artist were held in low esteem.

In his more pessimistic moments Audubon himself may have been inclined to agree with that low assessment of his work. He sometimes castigated himself for allowing the pure enjoyment and the personal satisfaction that he derived from bird painting to deflect him from the solid business of making money. But this was before he had the unforgettable experience of seeing Wilson's work. Now suddenly the chance encounter with Wilson opened up new vistas for him. The sight of Wilson's portfolios, with their competent representations of birds, revealed to Audubon for the first time the noble purpose of a systematic study of North American birds. As he feasted his eyes on Wilson's paintings, deep within him there stirred a half-formed wish to do something similar on his own. Similar? Yes, but superior to Wilson's work. He himself declares, as we have seen, that his vocation as a full-time naturalist was clearly revealed to him for the first time after a meeting in Philadelphia with Lucien Bonaparte, to whom he refers by his title of Prince of Musignano. But the meeting with Wilson was an earlier and more important catalyst. As he stood behind the counter in his store gazing at Wilson's pictures, he asked himself if he were not capable of undertaking a work of the same sort, or better still, one in which he might surpass the older naturalist as a painter of the birds of America.

By this time Audubon had become aware of his many shortcomings as a scientist and artist. He lacked systematic training in zoology. He knew little of scientific nomenclature, and he also realized that he was deficient in many of the techniques of painting. He was, for instance, unpracticed in the use of oils. As a painter he was entirely self-taught, with the many faults and few virtues of such a background. Yet something told him that while Wilson's birds were good, surprisingly good, his own, for the most part, were better. He tells us in his autobiography that he discovered the combination of watercolor and pastel that was to become his favorite medium quite by accident. He was painting in watercolor a miniature of Lucy before their marriage, when by mischance a drop of water fell on the face, dried there, and marred it horribly. Then he goes on: "After much labor to repair the damage I found the blur still remained. I resorted to a piece of colored chalk, applied it, rubbed the spot with a cork stump, and at once caught the desired effect."

Audubon was not yet in a position to desert retail business and devote himself fully to his painting, but from this time on he worked harder than ever. After the inevitable dull hours in the shop he went out to spend uncounted additional hours in the woods in pursuit of new specimens for his brush. He continually reviewed all the sketches he had and found many of them unsatisfactory. As already noted, he repainted every likeness that in any way displeased him.

He began also to learn the Latin names of the birds in order to assign them their place in the scheme of things. He was not ready to declare it to all comers or even to acknowledge it frankly to himself or his family, but the idea of becoming Audubon the Naturalist had taken root and was to continue to grow. He saw that he would have to add the consideration of migrations, color changes, and other important aspects of bird life to his studies. He was aware of these things already, but he would need to study them scientifically and methodically if he were to compete with the academicians already at work in the field. In contrast, from now on the petty affairs of Audubon, Rozier and Company took on more than ever an aspect of dead weight, and he begrudged more than ever the time he must spend on them. He felt increasingly that his time was better spent in the woods or at his easel.

But for the moment there was little choice. Audubon divided his time among his friends, his family, his business, and his undeclared vocation. And at the back of his mind, but moving gradually forward to occupy a prominent place in his consciousness, was the recollection of the crabbed old Scotsman and his remarkable collection of bird portraits.

# 6

# THE MOVE
# TO HENDERSON

ABOUT ONE HUNDRED twenty-five miles downriver from Louisville stood the little town of Henderson. Like its larger neighbor it was located on a bluff overlooking the Ohio. It was flanked by an extensive canebrake in which wild birds and animals teemed—a naturalist's paradise. Founded in 1792 by the Transylvania Land Company, the town had long been known as Red Banks, but it had recently been renamed in honor of Richard Henderson, the land company's prominent member. Rozier wished to move the firm to this location. He was disappointed in their progress in Louisville and discouraged by the growing competition. He suggested to Audubon that they close up the store they had been running for about two years and move downriver.

Rozier's arguments for the move were not very convincing. Having little of the pioneering spirit, he could not claim that like Boone, or Tom Lincoln, he wished to flee an influx of neighbors. Nor could he say truthfully that business was not good, but he tried to find plausible reasons for insisting that in a new place the partnership would make a more propitious start. As he had nothing better than a hunch to back up his arguments, Rozier's pleas sounded like specious reasoning, and neither Audubon nor his wife was much impressed by them. Louisville, as everyone could see, was growing rapidly, and there was every reason to believe that business would grow with it. Besides, Lucy Audubon had achieved in a very short time a most satisfactory circle of friends, both in the town and in Shippingport, and neither she nor her husband saw any compelling advantage in moving to a more remote location. To the contrary.

But in spite of his and Lucy's opposition, after a journey down the river to look the place over Audubon allowed himself to be persuaded. His reason for giving in so easily would not have impressed Rozier if he had known it, or had taken the trouble to find it out. Purely and simply Audubon realized that in their new location the country remained much wilder than in the vicinity of Louisville, and it would be sure to provide him with many new varieties of birds to sketch. Moreover Henderson was on a north-south bird flyway, and consequently wild birds of all kinds were far more numerous there than in the Louisville area. And in any case, as far as Audubon was concerned a shop was a shop; if he had to stand behind a counter and wait on trade, the need to do so in Henderson would prove neither more nor less irksome to him there than in Louisville. Thus on balance it was not Audubon, the supposedly restless wanderer, but Rozier, the steady man of affairs, who proposed and accomplished the move to Henderson.

When the decision had been made, the move was not really complicated. Audubon and Rozier had simply to load their entire stock of merchandise on a flatboat and head down the river toward Henderson. It is not certain how Lucy and little Victor were transported to their new home, but presumably they either accommodated themselves in the cramped quarters aboard the boat that held the firm's merchandise or came along afterward in some smaller and less heavily loaded river craft, perhaps a skiff.

Probably they rode in the flatboat, in view of the precarious state of the family finances. In any case the journey was not of long duration.

The wilderness town of Louisville had at first sight seemed somewhat unpromising to the city-bred Lucy. A little more than two years later Henderson in its turn looked hopelessly backward and uninviting, for in 1810 the place was a tiny outpost on the frontier. It was Audubon's subsequent recollection that when he settled there, Henderson consisted of but six or eight houses. In fact the village was much larger than that, for though the settlement was small, the county in which it was situated already boasted more than 4,500 inhabitants, according to the census of 1810. Not a few of the settlers were veterans of the Revolutionary War who had come to the West in the hope of finding low-priced, fertile land.

Once they had reached the town, the Audubons set up housekeeping in a log cabin standing not far from the river. It had been agreed among them that Rozier was to have room and board with them. The front part of the house was to serve as a store. Accounts of the first six or seven months that the Audubons spent in Henderson are lacking in intimate details of their life there, and we know nothing of their reactions to the place. We know but one thing for sure—that Lucy and her husband soon acquired a deep attachment to the local physician, Dr. Adam Rankin, who had moved his family from Louisville to Henderson as long ago as 1800. The doctor's wife, whom they met and liked, was his third, for his first two had been casualties of wilderness living, and remarriage in such instances was the usual and all but automatic procedure.

Whatever the other hardships of the place, Lucy would hardly have been lonesome in any event. On September 27 the Audubons went to board with the Rankins and their thirteen children, and later, when they finally set up their own establishment again, they had several boarders. This is shown by the census lists, which record as residents of their house not only Audubon, Lucy, and their son Victor, but also Rozier and the company clerk, Nathaniel Pope, who had come with them from Louisville.

One would have thought that under the circumstances Rozier would have considered himself well-off. He was well housed and ate home cooking with the family. But evidently he was not easily satisfied. Only a few months after they had arrived in Henderson, entirely at his urging, and when the new store had been stocked and open for business but a short while, he opened a campaign to belittle Henderson and urge his partner to move farther on, that is, either all the way to Saint Louis or to the nearly all-French town of Sainte Genevieve, some fifty miles up the Mississippi from the confluence of the Ohio and Mississippi rivers in what is now Missouri. As he had done when urging the previous move, he now alleged purely business reasons for his proposal. The fact that he and Lucy Audubon did not get along well together apparently had some bearing on the situation, though how a move would have improved their relationship is hard to say. Audubon, always ready for an excursion into new and unfamiliar territory, agreed to a joint expedition to look over the other towns with a particular view to their commercial possibilities. Audubon, in the account of his life addressed to his sons, thus describes Rozier's persuasive tactics:

Your blessed mother and I were as happy as possible; the people around loved us, and we them; our profits were enormous, but our sales small, and my partner suggested that we remove to Sainte Genevieve on the Mississippi River. I acceded to his request, but was quite determined to leave your mother and Victor in Henderson, not being quite sure that our venture would succeed as we hoped. I therefore placed her and the children [sic] under the care of Dr. Rankin, who had a fine farm about three miles from Henderson.

The discussions of a move farther west occurred in the late fall, when the weather was not at all propitious for a long journey on the river; but Rozier insisted. He wanted to load a boat and start at once. Again Audubon too good-naturedly agreed. Neither of the partners paid any heed to the fact that the dead of a wilderness winter was hardly the ideal time of year for a journey down an untamed river in a heavily loaded flatboat, or even to the fact that in setting out in a snowstorm on the twenty-second of December they were leaving Lucy and little Victor alone for the Christmas season. But Christmas may have seemed less important then than it does now, and certainly having to be often alone was thought of without apology as the inescapable lot of a wife on the frontier. It was easy, in any case, to arrange for Lucy and Victor to stay with the Rankins. Here Mrs. Audubon made herself useful to her host family as a tutor to their children—an occupation that was to serve her well in years to come.

Audubon's sudden decision to go off with Rozier was not an uncharacteristic gesture on his part. Throughout his life he was second to none in his affection for his family, but he could always rationalize an apparent need to separate himself from them for long and indefinite periods of time. And so with cheerful insouciance he left his wife and child on this wintry day to the generosity and lovingkindness of friends.

It was with few if any backward thoughts that Audubon and Rozier loaded their supplies and merchandise on a riverboat for their pioneering journey. They were well equipped for the voyage. Audubon said of their boat, "It was new, staunch and well trimmed, and had a cabin in her bow." They were accompanied by Nathaniel Pope, who seems to have been willing to follow them everywhere they went. They also employed two crewmen. The Ohio was still free of ice, and as long as their boatmanship consisted merely of guiding their craft around the curves and of helping it along now and then with oars, their progress was easy and somewhat faster than the speed of the current, which was about five miles an hour.

42

But when the party reached the confluence of the Ohio River and the Mississippi, their means of locomotion changed radically. Even rowing full strength against the strong current of the Mississippi was ineffectual. It now became necessary for each of the men in turn to go ashore and don a harness to tow the boat while walking the riverbank. "Pulling the cordella," they called it. Nor should anyone imagine that there was a well-defined tow path such as follows a barge canal. Towing a boat along the Mississippi, difficult enough along the somewhat cleared and civilized riverbank of today, must have been a stupendous and nearly impossible task in the early 1800s. But even this backbreaking chore could not keep Audubon's attention away from his surroundings and the wildlife to be found there. He records proudly, "While I was tugging with my back at the cordella, I kept my eyes fixed on the forest or the ground, looking for birds or curious shells." Progress each day was painfully slow, for the partners report that they thought ten miles a day, or just a little more than a mile an hour during daylight, a very fair achievement.

Yet even this snail's pace could not be kept up for long. Soon the drift ice began to accumulate along the shore in heaps ten to twenty feet high, and in a little while these barriers proved so formidable and so rough that all thought of forward progress had to be abandoned. The only possible course of action was to set up camp on shore, secure the boat some yards inland, far from possible incursions of moving ice, and then settle down to wait for the breakup that would come with the first spring thaw. These weeks of enforced idleness were a time of unmitigated torture to poor Rozier, and though one can sympathize with him, there is poetic justice in the thought that it was he, after all, who had insisted on setting out at such an unseasonable time of year. His plight amused Audubon who said of him: "Wrapped in a blanket like a squirrel in winter quarters with his tail about his nose, he slept and dreamed his time away, being seldom seen except at meals."

Audubon for his own part was not in the least intimidated by the cold and snow. Most days he left camp at daybreak to go hunting and was gone till dusk. In a short while he came to know the country around the camp like the palm of his hand. But with all his woodsman's expertise, he admits that he found it possible occasionally, in the manner of any less-experienced wanderer, to get lost in a snowstorm and find himself crossing and recrossing his own trail. Sometimes he went hunting alone, and sometimes he relied on the skills and the company of friendly parties of Osage and Shawnee Indians. They soon became his friends, and laughed excitedly at his portraits of them. They rewarded him for his sketches by showing him a host of new birds to fill his notebooks and by teaching him countless details about the birds and their habits.

Meantime the beleaguered travelers in camp had a plentiful but monotonous diet. After several weeks of eating wild fowl and game they recorded that they had become very tired of wild turkey breast. The stuff was so dry that they had to smear it with bear grease in order to get it down. But there was at least no danger of starving, and however dull the life in camp seemed, Audubon thoroughly enjoyed his forays into the woods from the beginning to the end of their stay.

Luckily the ice broke up early that year. After six weeks of camping on shore, there came a deafening crash and a roar that could be heard for miles. The travelers ran to their boat to save it from the grinding ice that invaded the riverbank. Then as rapidly as possible they broke camp and resumed their painful progress upstream, towing the boat from the shore by the cordella at about the same rate as before. The total distance from Henderson to Sainte Genevieve, then located within the jurisdiction of the Territory of Louisiana, was in the neighborhood of one hundred sixty-five miles, and the entire trip, including the enforced encampment, took some nine weeks in all. They arrived in Sainte Genevieve late in February.

What the party of Kentuckians came upon at the end of their strenuous and exhausting journey was a disappointingly wretched and primitive settlement, planted in the midst of a desolate and monotonous prairie; at least that was Audubon's jaundiced view, for he disliked the place on sight and said so. He characterized it as "not so large as ugly." The only stock-in-trade the partners had in abundance was a cargo of three hundred barrels of whiskey, which they had bought for twenty-three cents a gallon, and which, according to Audubon, they disposed of for two dollars a gallon. This is probably an exaggeration, for, as we shall see, Audubon was not strictly accurate in such statements. Aside from this single lucky and profitable deal Audubon could see no prospects, commercial or otherwise, that would induce him to move his family and resettle them in the ugly town, or go into retail business there.

Rozier, on the other hand, liked the place as readily as Audubon disliked it. He was convinced that the town had a great future. Socially he was at once at home among the French and French Canadians who made up the bulk of the population. In almost no time at all he, the unsociable one, met and started courting Constance Roy, a French Canadian girl about half his own age, whom he frankly said he intended to marry. He saw for himself every omen of the good life in the Mississippi River town whose French language and character were surely the real reasons for his enthusiasm. He declared to Audubon that he would go no farther. He would make his home in Sainte Genevieve and become the founder of a sizable family—a prophecy he was to fulfill, incidentally. Nathaniel Pope was also charmed by Sainte Genevieve and stated his intention to settle there with Rozier.

Audubon's feelings, as we have seen, were quite different. He made up his mind to return to Henderson and his family as soon as practicable. But Rozier refused to budge from his new home, and under the circumstances there was nothing to do but dissolve the partnership. This they proceeded to do forthwith. A formal paper was drawn up and the two men signed it April 6, 1811. By this contract Rozier became the sole owner of their joint enterprise, and since he had not sufficient funds available to reimburse Audubon in cash for his full share of the business, he arranged to pay off the balance in regular installments.

Thus occurred the final and definitive break in the commercial relations of the two men, but without any hint of ill feeling between them. The ending of their partnership was a simple solution of the problems resulting from their basic differences in point of view. Not only did the two men continue to see each other often in a casual way, but many years later when Audubon had become famous and Rozier was a wealthy old man, the merchant was a guest at Audubon's home on the Hudson River. Their sentiments regarding each other when they parted in Sainte Genevieve were certainly frank enough. Audubon said: "Rozier cared for money and liked Sainte Genevieve." Rozier riposted: "Audubon had no taste for commerce and was continually in the forest."

As to how Audubon made his way across country to his home in Henderson, there are two conflicting stories, both of them from his own pen, but written at different times. The variations to be found in the two accounts illustrate the extent to which Audubon's faulty memory could produce divergent accounts of simple happenings. According to one of these versions he simply took a compass bearing toward Henderson and struck out afoot through the woods on a beeline, living off the country and enjoying every minute of the excursion. His mood at the time is reflected in his euphoric description of the countryside: "The weather was fine, all around me was fresh and blooming as if it had just issued from the bosom of nature. My knapsack, my gun and my dog were all that I had for baggage and company. But although well mocassined, I moved slowly along, attracted by the brilliancy of the flowers, and the gambols of the fawns around their dams, to all appearances as thoughtless to danger as I felt myself."

According to the second account he bought a fine horse and rode home in style. Not that it matters much. We may be sure that in either case his stops to draw birds and observe wildlife were both frequent and profitable. He arrived back in Henderson on an April evening unannounced after an absence of some four months.

Without Rozier at his side to keep urging them to move on, the chances seemed good that Audubon and his family would remain in Henderson for an indefinite period. They had not been long there, but they felt themselves well established in the little community. Certainly Lucy Audubon was not the restless type. She had left Louisville reluctantly, agreeing to the move only at her husband's and Rozier's urging. What she had come to want for herself above all, no matter where she lived, was a comfortable, well-furnished home, and she began to plan for its creation. She knew from observing her friends' homes that a log cabin could be as tastefully furnished and as nice to live in as a brick mansion, and she made plans to acquire some stylish furniture as soon as the family budget would allow it.

The Audubons' immediate prospects for financial security looked uncertain. John James had to decide whether he would attempt to open another retail store, and if so, with what capital. To this end Rozier's regular installments on his debt were expected to contribute heavily. The Audubons were also anticipating, though quite in vain, that a fair sum would be paid to Lucy from her father's estate while he was still living. They knew that as early as 1810, or about the time they were contemplating the move to Henderson, William Bakewell had decided to put Fatland Ford up for sale, together with the land holdings adjacent to it, in order to divide the proceeds among his children. His reason for this premature liquidation is not clear, but the notably antagonistic attitude displayed by his second wife toward his children, and especially her active dislike of Lucy and her husband, may have contributed to the decision. Perhaps Bakewell feared that his widow might somehow be able to circumvent provisions of his will if he put off the distribution of his property until his death. In any case he had the proper papers drawn to put the farm up for sale. The sale was not immediately consummated, however, as only small parcels were disposed of, and the Audubons' share of these proceeds presumably dribbled in from time to time.

Actually the only real money that Audubon ever received from the East was the proceeds from his share in the Mill Grove Farm, which William Bakewell had disposed of for him in 1810. The sum due was $8,000, but this sum had several claims against it, including Bakewell's fee as agent, and it is not clear when Audubon received the money. But whenever they were forthcoming the payments must have been a welcome prop to his business and his usually shaky finances. Circumstances with him were generally such that he spent new money in anticipation of its being received. Thus at the moment a home of his own and a prosperous business were still wishes for the future.

On his return home from Sainte Genevieve, Audubon had found his wife still settled in the Rankins' home, teaching their children the ABC's and being treated as a beloved member of the family. With his characteristic hospitality Dr. Rankin was quick to tell Audubon to make his home with them until he knew for certain what his plans would be. And as usual, the naturalist had no difficulty in postponing a difficult decision. For him the breakup of the partnership his father had contrived came as a welcome release from bondage. For the moment he was content to make no plans; he rejoiced in his freedom and devoted himself to his favorite pursuits. For some weeks he and Lucy continued to live with the Rankins while Audubon spent his time in the woods or in his room drawing the birds he had captured or shot during his recent trip. It is to this temporarily carefree period of Audubon's life that we owe his drawings of the pewit, the great-crested flycatcher and the then numerous Carolina parrakeet.

Still, even Audubon knew that absolute leisure, free from all necessity of earning his own living, could not endure forever. Now that he no longer had Rozier to prod him, he knew that he would have to take upon himself the management of his own affairs. He must earn a living for his family, and as he considered the problem, he recognized ruefully that running a retail store was the only trade he had learned. Finally, he made up his mind to break into business again. To purchase merchandise he took a trip upriver to Louisville, which he found in a state of high prosperity. Pausing only briefly to see the Berthouds and his other old friends, he ordered supplies for his new venture, an act that in itself implies either a certain solvency or a fair credit rating.

As he floated back toward Henderson on the return trip, Audubon was glad that he had left the larger town behind. He discovered he had no wish to return there to live. He saw that Louisville was rapidly becoming a metropolis, and he had come to prefer to live in a smaller town. Years later he was to reflect philosophically that if he had stayed on in Louisville, its prosperity would surely have engulfed him. Caught in the toils of success, he would never have had the courage to break away from routine and strike out on his own. Affluence, in a word, would have destroyed his career as a naturalist.

# 7

# AUDUBON AND THOMAS BAKEWELL

IT WAS AT ABOUT this time, to Audubon's misfortune be it said, that Lucy's brother, Thomas Bakewell, stopped by to pay an unannounced visit. He was an enthusiastic, even visionary young man who had not yet found his niche in the world, and on his arrival in Henderson he was brimming over with plans and purposes and talking excitedly of his latest dream. He was on his way to New Orleans, where he proposed to set himself up as a commission merchant. He had heard tales of fortunes made rapidly, and he could hardly wait to get started. In a moment of exultation he invited Audubon to join him as a partner, prophesying brilliant success for the two of them. Audubon's French background and knowledge of the French language, he said frankly, would stand him in good stead in the half-French city. And a partnership between a Franco-American and an Anglo-American would be an unbeatable combination.

Audubon, to whom daydreams of affluence were still as attractive as ever, allowed himself to be cajoled into acceptance. Nor was Lucy slow to add her pleas to those of her brother. In her active imagination the southern city, with its reputation for gaiety and sophistication, would make a splendid change from the ruder towns of

Louisville and Henderson. After an evening of discussion Lucy and her brother won the day. With the decision made, Audubon sealed the agreement by agreeing to invest some of his money in the new firm, which was to be called Audubon and Bakewell. Audubon's enthusiasm was so great that he had some letterheads printed up the next day and sat down to write a letter on one of them to his old partner Rozier to tell him the good news. Bakewell was sped happily on his way south and the Audubons' hopes rode with him.

While they waited day after day in expectation of good news from New Orleans, Audubon thought a trip to Sainte Genevieve might be helpful. Rozier's remittances were not arriving with regularity, and a personal visit might result in a cash payment. On his arrival in the Mississippi River town Audubon found his old partner changed. He was far more expansive now than he had been. He was happily married, and he proclaimed loudly to Audubon that his business was flourishing; but when pressed for a payment on account he was embarrassed to admit ruefully that most of his assets were not liquid, and that he had little or no ready cash at his disposal. He made excuses, saying what Audubon already knew—that on the frontier so many payments were received in kind that a merchant's assets, though real enough, were not always in transferable form. Audubon congratulated him on his success but had to return home with nothing to show for his journey.

That same fall of 1811, Audubon (who thought nothing at all of a five- or six-hundred-mile journey across country) decided that before the projected move to New Orleans he would take the family to Philadelphia for a visit. In view of the strained relations between the Bakewells and himself this decision can only appear to have been a foolish one, and so it turned out. The plan to have Lucy and little Victor spend the winter in the same house with Lucy's stepmother did not arouse happy thoughts on either side. But Audubon was always optimistic. Brushing aside all obstacles, he was positive he could simply leave his family at Fatland Ford and go off alone to New Orleans. Once there he fully expected to find Audubon and Bakewell's affairs flourishing. He would then send for his wife in a matter of weeks, and they would be happily reunited in Louisiana.

As might have been foreseen, Lucy's reception at the Perkiomen farm was not a cordial one, though her father was glad to see her. Rebecca Smith Bakewell showed herself as disagreeable as ever to all concerned. Salutations had barely been exchanged when Audubon was rudely taxed with his failure to repay a debt he owed the family. Old William Bakewell was but a shadow of his former self—quite unable to stand up for his daughter and son-in-law. He was in poor spirits, and his health was failing visibly. This being so, the prospect of a long stay in Philadelphia looked grim indeed to Lucy. Far better, she thought, a happy though simple life on the frontier than a sojourn in this cold household that had once been her home.

It was during the Audubons' absence from Henderson that a notable event occurred: the arrival in town of the first steamboat on the Ohio River. It was one of Robert Fulton's boats, the *New Orleans,* and its appearance titillated the entire population along the Ohio and Mississippi rivers. Up to this time the existence of the new type of river craft was known about and spoken of in Henderson, but no one had actually seen one. The fact of Audubon's absence from home disposes once and for all of the legend that while the boat was tied up at the dock in Henderson, Audubon dived under one side of the hull and came up on the other side. Such a stunt would certainly have been in character, creature of impulse that he was; and as to swimming in and across the Ohio River, both Audubon and his wife were especially fond of such exercise, which they often indulged in before breakfast. But plausible as the story seems, it simply was not true.

Instead the Audubons found themselves a thousand miles from Henderson.

Although it was apparent that the situation in her father's house was to be little more than bearable, it was decided after some discussion that Lucy and Victor would remain there. In the meantime Audubon would travel west and south, passing through Henderson on the way. He was mounted on his famous wild horse, Barro, of which he was enormously proud. He had purchased him in a semiwild state and had tamed him to the point where he could not only let Lucy ride him but had told her she could consider the horse her own.

This trip west was to prove rich in anecdotes useful to Audubon in his "episodes," as he called his tales of life on the frontier. The first of these incidents, which he later would publish in his *Ornithological Biography,* was occasioned by his meeting with an interesting traveler in the person of Vincent Nolte. This gentleman, who was but one of the numerous persons of European background who roamed America in search of adventure, was a German born in Leghorn, Italy. At the time he and Audubon met, in December 1811, Nolte was what the naturalist aspired to become, a commission merchant in New Orleans. Their meeting took place at an overnight stop at a country inn somewhere between Harrisburg and Pittsburgh, near the Juniata River. In the dining room Nolte was glancing about when his eye fell upon a stranger of striking appearance who was seated near him. On impulse he called out to him to ask if he were a Frenchman. In reply Audubon, for it was he, being in one of the waggish moods that so often overtook him, replied with the strongest French accent he could muster "No, Saire, Hi Ham an Eengleeshman." After the laughter had died down, Nolte invited the stranger to join him at his table, which Audubon agreed to do. It did not take the German long to find out that his interlocutor, though fond of clowning, was decidedly a man of parts, and so after an evening agreeably spent in each other's company they decided to travel together the next morning.

Their immediate goal was Pittsburgh, but, when they got there, the town proved to be in a state of furious activity. Audubon consequently, though he tried for several days, could find no available transportation downriver. Hearing of his plight, his new friend generously offered him passage on one of his own boats. Audubon accepted with thanks. Their horses were to follow them on a flatboat lashed behind their own: thus the two companions could continue to travel together. Both being men of infinite curiosity and wide experience—of which they loved to talk—they enlivened the journey by the recital of their remarkable and amusing adventures. Thus the time passed quickly, for Audubon and Nolte were as at home in each other's company as if they had been friends for years.

At Maysville, Kentucky, which was then a small village called Limestone, the travelers disembarked to continue their journey on horseback across country. When they reached Lexington, Audubon rode on alone in the direction of Frankfort, leaving Nolte to find his way unaccompanied.

Following well-known trails toward Frankfort, Louisville, and Henderson, Audubon rode on, still mounted on Barro. He was not long gone from Lexington when the second notable event of his journey occurred. Barro was an intelligent horse and needed little guidance, and Audubon was deep in his own thoughts, probably dreaming of financial success in New Orleans, when a notable natural catastrophe occurred. Throughout the region a violent earth tremor was felt, terrifying the people of the settlements not only in central Kentucky, where Audubon then was, but even in Henderson and in the neighborhood of the Rankins at Meadow Brook Farm. Audubon has related the story of this upheaval in another of his episodes, entitled "The Earthquake." He tells us that when he first noticed the tremor, Barro, who was usually afraid of nothing, simply spread his feet wide apart, disobeyed all commands, and refused to budge. Frantic efforts by Audubon to make him move were of no avail. Meanwhile from everywhere and yet from nowhere came the awesome rumblings that accompanied the quake. Motionless, man and horse stood as if riveted to the spot. Barro, obviously, would move only when he judged it safe to do so.

It was a terrifying experience, but Audubon as usual recovered his courage quickly. Later when he cast his mind back over the incident, he saw it principally as grist for his literary mill. This was the sort of tale about the wilds of America that European readers found so fascinating. And Audubon, the author of *Birds of America,* was not unaware of the value of anecdotes in drawing attention to his book. He also perceived that potential purchasers liked to look toward the man behind the book, the woodsman who was so different from the usual European scientist.

When Audubon reached Henderson the daydreams of success in which he had been indulging himself as he rode along the trail were dashed summarily to the ground. He found there a message from his new partner, Thomas Bakewell, who wrote in an extremely discouraging vein. He related to Audubon that his inquiries in the southern city had resulted in a total pessimism. Even his youthful enthusiasm could see no prospects for business success. In commercial circles there was widespread uncertainty. The Embargo Act had already brought trade to a standstill. On top of this there was now the imminent war against England to be reckoned with, and this conflict promised to render foreign trade all but impossible. At the same time Audubon suffered another disappointment in finding no word for him from Rozier. As usual he had hoped for money from him, possibly even enough to clear up his partner's remaining one thousand dollars of debt. In any event Rozier had promised to write but had failed to do so. In view of these disappointments Audubon saw little use in proceeding to New Orleans or even as far as Sainte Genevieve. The only sensible course of action was to return to Philadelphia and bring his family back with him to Kentucky, and this he set out to do.

Once reunited with Lucy at Fatland Ford, Audubon made no move to set out for home as Lucy expected him to do, with the atmosphere in her father's house so tense. He rested for a while instead, indulging himself in excursions in the nearby woods, of which he was particularly fond. As was his custom he drew birds. His young brother-in-law, William, captured a hawk and brought it to him unharmed. He sketched this bird, though he was disappointed at its docility, and when his work was done, released it from the window.

It was during this same stay that he paid his visit to the studio of Alexander Wilson. He admits that the old man was not cordial, but I think it may be reasonably argued from the fact that he took the trouble to look him up at all that the personal relations between the two ornithologists were not nearly so antagonistic as painted in the account printed by George Ord. Still, the churlish remarks in Wilson's diary, which Audubon seemingly took at face value, appear to have rankled, for years later in the third volume of his *Ornithological Biography*, Audubon took up the subject of Wilson again, writing as much in sorrow as in anger: "Louisville, State of Kentucky, March 1810. I had the gratification of taking Alexander Wilson to some ponds within a few miles of town, and of showing him many birds of this species [Whooping Crane] of which he had not previously seen any other than stuffed specimens. I told him that the white birds were the adults, and that the grey were the young. Wilson in his article on the Whooping Crane has alluded to this, but, as on other occasions, he has not informed his readers whence his information came."

The war with Britain—Mr. Jefferson's war, as the New England antiwar party called it—had formally begun on June 18, 1812, and Audubon had begun to think of returning to Kentucky. Meanwhile, on the Fourth of July the same year, he went before a naturalization court in Philadelphia to become an American citizen. Three weeks later he and his family began their homeward journey, accomplishing the river portion of it in a barge belonging to their friend William Clark. The explorer had offered the use of his boat to any Kentuckian westward bound in order to help him get home before the actual outbreak of hostilities with Britain, expected to touch all parts of the United States including the western frontier. In Louisville the Audubons counted on their friend Berthoud for transportation farther down the river in one of his boats, but for reasons best known to himself Berthoud made them no offer, and so they had to return to Henderson in a rented skiff.

Nor were their personal financial troubles and the failure of their plans for moving to New Orleans the only preoccupations of the Audubon family. For one thing Lucy was pregnant again and desperately anxious to be in a home of their own for the birth of her child. For another, Audubon the artist was distressed to discover that a portfolio of more than two hundred finished drawings that he had left in a chest were ruined. As he put it: "A pair of Norway rats had reared a young family among the bits of paper that a few months ago represented over a thousand inhabitants of the air." For a few days he was inconsolable. Then as his habitual optimism reasserted itself, he remarked good-humoredly that with a bit of concentrated effort he would be able to do more than merely duplicate the ruined drawings; he would recreate them with the newer and better techniques he had acquired since his first attempts were made. He was inclined to feel that what at first had looked like a tragic loss was a blessing in disguise. In a matter of three years, indeed, he had reconstituted his collection.

It was at this juncture, in August 1812, just after their return to the home of the Rankins, that young Thomas Bakewell walked in, again unannounced, with the unwelcome news that the partnership he had tried to organize in New Orleans was a total failure and that the money the Audubons had invested had been lost in an out-and-out bankruptcy. What to do? Another evening of discussion took place, this one more pessimistic than the last. At length Audubon, unwisely as it turned out, invited Thomas to remain with them in Henderson to become a partner in some sort of business.

Several months later, on November 30, 1812, Lucy gave birth to their second son, John Woodhouse. A sickly child he proved to be, whose life was often despaired of. But as the years passed, he outgrew his ailments to become an artist whose talents were often helpful to his father. On the very day of his birth Audubon painted the great American shrike.

Lucy Audubon's desire to have a home of her own was rendered more acute by the presence now of two children, which made a longer stay at the Rankins impractical. Securing a house was not easy in a village as small as Henderson, but a lucky chance put in their way a comfortable one-and-a-half-story cabin about a block from the river. This dwelling was to be the Audubons' home for no less than seven years; in it they experienced struggle and even failure, but also great happiness.

To improve the land and render it more useful Audubon dug a good-sized pond adjacent to the cabin. This he stocked with fish and even a few turtles, which were expected to provide the table with soup. On the surface of the pond swam a covey of ducks, some of them wild. There was also a wild turkey that stayed around and became known to everyone in town. The land was planted with a large orchard. The new store was next to the house and well stocked with merchandise. Lucy went to work to furnish the house, and in time she put together a most satisfactory collection of necessary articles.

Audubon's purchase of a house was related to several other land purchases that he made in the town. He bought two one-acre lots for $600 in 1813 and two more the following year. He also took a ninety-nine year lease on some land near the river. All these purchases are a matter of record, but it may be said in passing that in discussing them Audubon sometimes became confused, and his written recollections are at variance with the facts. Some time later Audubon managed to sell his holdings at a profit, disproving the thesis sometimes advanced that he was never a good man of business. It now appears that during the early years of the partnership with Thomas Bakewell his business flourished and he enjoyed the greatest prosperity of his younger days. He himself said, "The little stock of goods brought from Louisville answered so perfectly that in less than twelve months I had again risen in the world."

Audubon was not so absorbed in business that he forgot his interest in birds. It was during 1813 that Audubon described for posterity one of the great natural wonders of the new world, now gone forever: the mighty flocks of passenger pigeons in their migrations. Audubon first saw this sight from the veranda of Young's Inn in the vicinity of West Point, Kentucky. He described them as a horde so vast that it darkened the sky and took several days to pass. Hunters in the neighborhood, and all those who could possibly reach the area where the pigeons were passing, indulged in an orgy of killing which Audubon describes in detail. No one foresaw then, not even Audubon, that this ruthless killing of the passenger pigeons would in a short time bring about their total extinction.

Henderson was growing. New businesses were starting up and new houses were being built. Dr. Rankin, among others, decided to move in from the country and built himself a splendid brick house not far from the Audubons. Thomas Bakewell had a house built nearby also, but instead of moving into it he preferred to live with his sister and partner.

The development of the land around the cabin, and the furnishing of its interior, was a labor of love for the

Audubons. For the first time Lucy had a home of which she could be proud. Years later Audubon was to write enthusiastically of those days. "The pleasure that I felt at Henderson and under the roof of that log cabin can never be effaced from my heart until after death."

In later years, when fame finally came to him, Audubon was sometimes pleased to look back and reflect upon lost opportunities. He had been tempted to invest in Louisville land, he said, and had failed to do so. In retrospect he was inclined to regard the opportunity as well lost. He wrote: "We marked Louisville as a spot designed by nature to become a place of great importance, and had we been as wise as we now are, I might never have published the *Birds of America;* for a few hundred dollars laid out, at that period, in lands or town lots near Louisville, would, if left to grow over with grass to a date ten years past [1835], have become an immense fortune, but young heads are on young shoulders; it was not to be, and who cares?"

During these relatively prosperous days the firm of Audubon and Bakewell decided to open a branch store, to be located in Shawneetown, Illinois, thirty miles downriver from Henderson. For manager of the new store they chose a man named David Apperson. About him not much is known except that he was an excellent man for the job, judging by the results. The agreement was signed in January 1814, and was so successful that it was renewed until January 1, 1817. Apperson was to receive a third of the profits, which were not inconsiderable. While the outlet was in business, he turned over to Audubon and Bakewell the sum of $6,402.

The most ambitious of the firm's undertakings, and one of which they were at first very proud, was the construction of a saw- and gristmill on the land that Audubon had leased on the riverbank. As it turned out, the mill was far from successful and was largely instrumental in dragging Audubon into bankruptcy. This mill, a huge and ugly structure as can be seen from pictures of it, was to outlast Audubon by many years and to remain a landmark in the town of Henderson. In fact the old mill would probably still be standing today, so sturdily was it built, had it not been destroyed by fire in 1913, more than sixty years after the naturalist's death. Its place has been taken by a public park where picnickers now view the river from the mill site where Audubon and Bakewell labored.

The initiative in this second undertaking of the partnership also came from Bakewell. The young man had allowed himself to become permeated with optimism about the commercial needs of Henderson County. He decided, without troubling to investigate, that the town was in urgent need of a saw- and gristmill. He and Audubon would build one and grow rich. Audubon once again was convinced. Neither of the partners thought of ascertaining the amount of wood to be sawed or grain to be milled. Their plans, therefore, had little to do with reality. With the benefit of hindsight Audubon sums up: "Unfortunately for me, he took it into his brain to persuade me to erect a steam mill at Henderson. Up went the mill at an enormous expense in a country as unfit for such a thing as it would be now for me to attempt to settle on the moon."

Once the construction of the mill had been decided upon, the partners pushed ahead rapidly with their plans. They enlisted the aid of Thomas Pears, a friend and neighbor of Lucy's father who had helped in the construction of a threshing machine for use on the Fatland Ford Farm. Pears, when appealed to, was more than willing to come to their assistance, lured probably by the prospect of becoming a full partner in the mill and thus having a one-third share in its profits, which he supposed would be enormous. He lost no time in selling his farm in Pennsylvania and came immediately to Henderson to look over the ground. His reaction was unfavorable. He was terribly disappointed by what he saw and regretted having acted hastily, but he resisted the temptation to turn back. His first step was to go fetch his numerous family. While in Philadelphia he persuaded a mechanic named Prentice to come along with him and assume responsibility for building the power plant.

Matters got off to a somewhat dismal start. In the first place, Audubon, Bakewell, and Pears did not adjust very well to each other. They continually disagreed on fundamentals. In the second place, the progress of construction was most uneven. There was also the important fact that Thomas Bakewell and his new bride were living with the Audubons—a fatal mistake, for Eliza did not see eye to eye with Lucy on housekeeping matters, and naturally Thomas took his wife's part. Pears and his family also expected to take their meals with the Audubons. The result was simply too much togetherness among a group of ill-assorted persons. Quarrels were frequent. Harsh words were exchanged. For an added complication Lucy was pregnant once more. Her child, a little girl named Lucy after her mother, was sickly and died two years later in 1817. Decidedly the Audubons were passing through a strenuous period.

The articles of agreement between the three partners in the mill also left much to be desired from Audubon's point of view; yet after discussion he seems to have agreed to them, although reluctantly. Bakewell and Pears were each to put up $4,000. This sum young Bakewell obtained painlessly by borrowing from his father. Pears used money derived from the sale of his farm. Audubon alone had to find the money somewhere among current assets. He was expected to assume the lion's share of the costs, or $7,000, to make up a total of $15,000. Out of this capital Prentice was to be paid a lump sum of $4,000 for building a sixteen-horsepower steam engine to run the mill.

The construction of the power plant would have been no easy task even for an expert, and Prentice's qualifications were not at that level. From the beginning he ran into an endless series of problems that would have plagued anyone trying to build so complicated a piece of machinery in a village so far from a center of population.

Though all the indispensable parts had supposedly been delivered to Henderson from the East before actual construction began, certain omissions were discovered daily. Only a few of the missing components could be improvised by Prentice's skill out of local materials. The usual procedure was to order what was needed from the East, sending messages by a passing river packet. Delays and frustrations were, therefore, inevitable. The estimated time for completing the job had to be doubled and redoubled, and costs ran far above the original budget. At last the engine ran, but it soon disappointed its owners. It was terribly inefficient and constantly breaking down. Prentice, of course, was blamed for all the engine's shortcomings, and the unfavorable consensus of the partners is expressed in Bakewell's words: "[Mr. Prentice] is a capital man to describe, but not to administer—his professional advice and opinions are invaluable, but his execution [is] worthless."

To provide lumber for the construction of his mill and a source of timber later, Audubon purchased 1,200 acres of wooded government land. Here too he encountered unexpected difficulties. To harvest his timber crop, cut it up, and deliver it to the mill site, Audubon had hired a company of itinerant Yankees then camped on the riverbank in the vicinity of Henderson. They appeared pleased to get the job and were provided by Audubon with all the necessary tools. The men began work at once and for a few days made good progress. Then suddenly one day the pack of dishonest ruffians skipped town, taking with them a yoke of oxen belonging to Audubon as well as all the tools he had provided for the job. Audubon was both aghast and furious. Rumor had it that the thieves had headed downstream, and Audubon set out at once in pursuit. But the fugitives were never captured nor the tools recovered.

The loss of the tools and particularly of the team of oxen was a blow to an already bedeviled enterprise, but finally the mill stood completed, in all its ugliness, on the appointed spot. A description of the building from one who had seen its does not flatter it much: "The original mill covered forty-five by sixty-five feet, and consisted of four stories and basement; the basement walls of stone stood four feet thick, while at the third story the thickness was three feet; the three upper stories were in frame. The studding measured three by six, and the rafters four by eight inches. Many of the large timbers that could then be seen were sound and apparently good for a century or more."

For a time it looked as if the huge but inefficient mill would be moderately successful in spite of its defects. The community welcomed its facilities. One of its first customers was the newly organized bank of Henderson, which purchased there the lumber for its new building. Its management also turned to another Audubon enterprise for bricks. But these orders were not followed up by enough others, and the mill never knew true success. It was too big and too inefficient for the place and time, and none of the partners was sufficiently patient to bide his time and wait for results, which might have come in due course. All three had counted on immediate profits.

In a short while both Pears and Bakewell, in succession, withdrew from the partnership, disappointed at its failure to make them rich. Prentice, judging by his nonchalant behavior throughout the construction, had been only moderately interested in the success of the undertaking from the start, considering himself a mere salaried employee (a well-paid one for the times, it may be observed). While supposedly working full time on the construction of the mill power plant, he had found the leisure to build and launch a steamboat.

When Thomas Bakewell finally made up his mind to withdraw from the partnership, he drove a hard bargain. On quitting Henderson with his disgruntled bride he told Audubon that he expected to be paid $5,500 for his share in the mill, either in a lump sum (which he knew to be beyond Audubon's means) or in five annual installments of $1,100 each. He also persuaded Prentice (despite his poor opinion of him) to leave with him. The two later became partners in what was to become a very successful shipbuilding business in Cincinnati.

After the collapse of the partnership Audubon operated the mill by himself for a while, but with no more than indifferent success. Finally in 1830, some years after he had ceased to live in Kentucky, the mill and its management were taken over by a new partnership under the name of J. J. Audubon and Company. On the surface this would appear to have afforded a viable solution, but Audubon always felt that his interest in the property had not been properly protected. He believed also that everyone except Lucy's brother-in-law, Nicholas Berthoud, who was a member of the caretaker-partnership, had taken unfair advantage of him. His summary of his feelings about the mill and its unsuccessful operation found expression in the following bitter words, written in retrospect: "The times were bad, but I am fully persuaded that the great fault was ours. How I labored in that accursed mill! But it is all over now; I am old and try to forget as fast as possible all the different trials of those sad days."

Yet amidst all the trials that beset him as a businessman, throughout the period of his association with his brother-in-law, when both he and his wife were rendered unhappy by having to make of their cabin a boarding-house for a group of ungrateful friends, associates, and relatives, Audubon never forsook his pursuit of wild birds, and while his troubles increased, so did the number of drawings in his portfolios.

# 8

# PICARESQUE ENCOUNTERS

INSEPARABLE FROM ANY consideration of Audubon's early career, and corresponding more or less precisely with his Kentucky years, is the story of his relationship with several picaresque characters and his participation in no few equally picturesque events. Interesting too is the varied and skillful use he made of both in his narratives. To understand this fully we must anticipate his later career a bit and realize that the image of the frontiersman that Audubon projected of himself in the eastern United States and in England was all part of his campaign to sell his great book. During his travels to acquire subscribers he chose the appearance of the woodsman deliberately: hence the unshorn locks and accouterments of the forest dweller that he took into the drawing rooms of potential subscribers. The dancer, the violinist, and the swordsman of France and Mill Grove were by no means forgotten, but merely laid aside. He thought a picturesque appearance would be a decided asset to his campaign for the sale of subscriptions to the *Birds of America.*

From the same motive came the tales he told. Everything that Audubon wrote had some basis in fact or experience, but in the telling he sometimes allowed himself to wander away from the plain, unvarnished truth. There is evidence that as he composed some of his "episodes" he deliberately made romantic stories out of fairly mundane events. He enjoyed adding the spice of suspense and danger when he thought the addition might improve the narrative. For this he was attacked by unfriendly critics, who said that his bird pictures were as exaggerated as his prose and no more to be relied upon. This was not true, of course, as any competent ornithologist now knows. But Audubon gave ammunition to his enemies by the tendency, which he did not try to resist, to tamper a bit with the truth.

Audubon also allowed his careless handling of the facts to carry over into his limited attempts at autobiography. There is, for instance, available for our inspection the written record of most of his business transactions, and over against that record we have Audubon's inaccurate recollections. The careful reader also notes that his own accounts of one and the same event furnished on separate occasions often vary significantly. Was this inaccuracy necessary or justifiable? To answer the question we must remind ourselves that while in some instances Audubon was seeking a calculated effect, at other times he was merely reacting as a poet for whom details of this kind were boring. When he wrote down (especially long after the fact) what he had felt and seen on a given occasion, he made little attempt at a pedantic or literal consistency.

An equally trying aspect of Audubon's writing, especially for the literal-minded reader, is his puckish sense of humor, which reveals itself at the most unlikely, even inopportune moments. A conspicuous example, already alluded to, is his facetious answer to Nolte in response to a question regarding his nationality.

There is a story told of Audubon that he once left his family for the east close-cropped and clean-shaven and returned several months later long-haired, with a full beard, and dressed in the uniform of a sailor in the French navy. The odd and the unusual had a strange attraction for him, and akin to this trait was a positive fondness for the originals and strong characters of his time. It is altogether understandable that he felt drawn to Daniel Boone. He relates that he once spent a night with Boone, and while they lodged together he induced the old scout to tell him about a famous Indian fight. This story he retold at a later date, for all stories, all anecdotes, were in the public domain as far as he was concerned. Boone was already an old man at the time of their meeting, but he was the best of the woodsmen and Audubon greatly admired him. They had much in common despite differences in background and education. Before he left Kentucky, he writes, he tried to arrange another hunting party with Boone, sending word downriver that if Boone were agreeable he would enjoy another meeting with him. But it was not to be. To Audubon's invitation Boone replied that he was failing in health, his eyes were growing dim, and he would have to leave such pleasures to his son.

One of Audubon's most exciting stories, which he entitled "A Night of Horror," is a sample of the sort of macabre tale that he sometimes achieved by adding a bit of literary artistry to an actual occurrence. According to the story as he published it, he was on his way back to Henderson from Sainte Genevieve in the spring of 1812 when at nightfall he asked for shelter overnight in a lone cabin. The woman occupant, an unprepossessing slattern, grudgingly assented and Audubon went inside. There he saw a badly wounded Indian, who indicated by signs that the woman was not to be trusted. In spite of his warning Audubon made the mistake of consulting his watch, which the woman openly coveted.

Audubon and the Indian prepared for the night, but in a short while the two stalwart sons of the household came home, carrying a stag between them. From the demeanor of the mother, who had just sharpened a knife, and of the sons, who had their firearms at the ready, Audubon and the Indian felt sure they were about to be murdered. Audubon confesses that at that moment he was as close to being afraid as he had ever been in his life. Just as the three ruffians were about to make their move, two strangers appeared in the doorway and rescued the intended victims. The owners of the cabin, says Audubon, were dealt with in the usual manner—that is, according to the retributive justice of the frontier they were beaten, their goods were forfeited, and their cabin was set on fire.

What shall we think of this story? It is well told. Certainly such an attack as the one described could have taken place. The stranger or traveler in the woods often depended for shelter and sustenance upon isolated settlers, yet despite the usually kindly disposition of the lone dweller in the forest, the bodies of murdered and unidentifiable persons were sometimes found. Renegades of the frontier, like the white man Simon Girty, and his Indian counterparts, were horrible exceptions to the prevailing tradition of hospitality. The cruelty of the renegades toward their victims is well documented. But did this particular incident occur just as Audubon tells it? It has been doubted, particularly on the basis of the supposed anachronism of the large whetstone said to have been used by the mother. Whether or not such an object existed on the frontier, the discussion seems academic to the modern reader. But in Audubon's day, when his every statement about a bird was subject to scrutiny on two continents, the accuracy of his tall tales was used as evidence for or against his general veracity as an ornithologist. For us the tale has appeal, and if it be merely the retelling of an ordinary event with the unpleasantness invented, what of that?

The use of the first-person narrative in this and many another of Audubon's stories added a measure of realism, and since he shrewdly realized how avid the public was for "true" tales of the wilderness, he capitalized on his skills. Excitement and thrills have never driven away readers, and Audubon often added these elements in the telling of otherwise ordinary occurrences which, in his hands, become high adventure.

This is not to say that unpleasant episodes had always to be invented. They not uncommonly happened. On at least two occasions, when Audubon was simply walking about within the limits of the village of Henderson, he was called upon to prove his courage against itinerant troublemakers. One of these fellows, a mean-spirited stranger, came walking into town one day with a vicious dog at his heels and the boast on his lips that his cur could lick all comers, whether man or beast. Audubon seems to have found the man blocking his path, and picking up a tree limb that lay at his feet he gave the dog a blow on the nose that sent him and his quarrelsome owner away with their tails between their legs.

On another occasion Audubon had to defend himself from a slightly more pretentious but no less obnoxious brawler, who walked into town and spoke Audubon's name specifically. He had heard that a man named Audubon fancied himself a swordsman, he said, and he wished to give him an opportunity to prove his skill. He thereupon challenged Audubon to a duel and called upon him to defend himself. Though usually a peaceful man in word and deed, Audubon decided reluctantly that he could not avoid the challenge, however silly and outrageous it seemed. Thereupon he went to fetch his sword. Assuming the position of the swordsman he needed but one well-aimed thrust to send his challenger sprawling. Picking himself up, the brawler left Henderson in a hurry.

More consequential contacts with his fellow men, many of them out of the ordinary, were the joy and diversion of Audubon's life, for Audubon was nothing if not gregarious. He was always meeting and talking to people, and he trusted them until he found reason for not doing so. Many of these total strangers later became his good friends. Sometimes he traveled with acquaintances for long distances and sometimes he merely greeted strangers on the trail, but he was never at a loss for words. Often, to Lucy's mingled annoyance and delight, he went so far as to invite the strangers he encountered to spend the night in his house. It was in 1818, toward the end of his sojourn in Kentucky, that a strange-looking gentleman presented himself to Audubon with a letter of introduction from his friends the Tarascons, at Shippingport. This traveler was Constantine Rafinesque, a naturalist born in Constantinople of a French father and a Greek mother. He had already paid several visits to America, and during this trip to Kentucky he was in search of new flora and fauna along the Ohio River and adjacent lands. The letter from Tarascon said, in part, "I send you a queer fish!" and Rafinesque good-humoredly admitted that the queer fish was undoubtedly himself. Audubon gives this account of their meeting: "One day while walking by the river I noticed a man landing with what I took to be a bundle of dry clover on his back. 'What an odd looking fellow, how the boatmen stare at him. Surely he must be an original,' said I to myself. He ascended the banks with rapid steps, then asked if I could point out the house where Mr. Audubon lived. 'Why I am the man and will gladly lead you to my house,' I replied."

Later Audubon gives this more detailed description of Rafinesque:

At table his agreeable conversation made us all forget his singular appearance. . . . A long loose coat of yellow nankeen, much the worse of the many rubs it had got in its time, and stained all over with the juice of plants, hung loosely about him like a sack. A waistcoat of the same, with enormous pockets, and buttoned up to the chin, reached below over a pair of tight pantaloons, the lower parts of which were buttoned down to his ankles. His beard was as long as I have known mine to be during some of my peregrinations, and his lank black hair hung loosely over his shoulders. His forehead was so broad and prominent that any tyro in phrenology would instantly have pronounced it to be the residence of a mind of strong powers. His words impressed an assurance of rigid truth, and as he directed the conversation to the study of natural sciences, I listened to him with as much delight as Telemachus could have listened to Mentor.

The Audubons entertained Rafinesque for several days. But noting a certain naïveté in him, Audubon spent one evening after his guest had retired in making drawings of outlandish and fanciful fish and fowl. These sketches he quietly showed to Rafinesque the next morning, assuring him solemnly that he had seen these denizens of the wilds on his rambles. Rafinesque was wholly taken in and declared himself delighted with the exhibits. Audubon's hospitality also included an intentionally trying excursion through an all but impossible canebrake. Rafinesque emerged exhausted and disheveled, while the amused Audubon was hardly out of breath. In a way Rafinesque evened the score, for on the last night of his stay he awoke Audubon long after he had gone to bed by making a tremendous row in his room. When Audubon went to investigate he found his guest running around his room in the buff, swatting at flying bats with no other weapon than Audubon's favorite and fairly valuable violin.

In telling this tale of the two naturalists, some biographers express disapproval of what they call Audubon's meanness and bad taste in having fun at the expense of his guest, however odd or naïve. The upshot was especially bad, they say, because Rafinesque took his host at his word and published drawings of some of the monstrosities furnished by Audubon as actual creatures of this world. Moreover he was careful to attribute them to his Henderson host. I suggest, however, that their sympathy is both exaggerated and misplaced, for Rafinesque (who a year later became a professor at Transylvania College in Lexington) often talked about his visit to Audubon, and always with affection and respect for the artist. Evidently he could take a joke and bore no grudge.

Rafinesque was not the only recipient of Audubon's practical jokes. The naturalist himself relates with mingled gusto and regret how he deluded a greenhorn from Europe into thinking the skunk a sort of tame squirrel.

The results can be imagined, and Audubon admits that he suffered almost as much as his victim; for since they were traveling together, there was no way of avoiding his company.

Another character to whom Audubon had offered hospitality was a swashbuckling Spanish nobleman. He was but one more of the odd wanderers of all European classes and countries who met and mingled on the American frontier. In fact for many years a trip to the wilds of North America was regarded as an essential ingredient in a man's career. This particular gentleman called himself General Don José Alvárez de Toledo y Dubois. He and Audubon met on the Ohio River between Louisville and Henderson. The "general" hailed Audubon from his boat and received a friendly reply. Having thus struck up a shouting acquaintance, the Spaniard and the Kentuckian lashed their boats together and floated downstream, talking and exchanging ideas. When they reached Henderson, nothing would do but that Audubon must take his new friend home to dinner and offer him hospitality for the night.

The next morning, as a reward for his kindness the Spaniard gave his host an ornamented dagger, and to Lucy Audubon he presented a ring. Then before leaving, the "general" made Audubon what sounded like a bona fide offer of employment. "Come with me to Mexico," he said. "[It is] a province ripe for the taking. . . . I will make you my associate with the rank of colonel." Audubon's imagination was not in the least kindled by the prospect of a life of military adventure. As a teen-age boy he had left France in the first place to avoid the recruiters of Napoleon, and he had never been sorry. Now he saw no reason to change his mind. All he could do was to decline the offer with thanks while he kindly directed the general to some of the town loafers who might be induced, in the hope of booty and three square meals a day, to enlist in a private army. The self-styled general left town and it was soon after discovered that he was a triple agent, engaged in spying for James Monroe as well as for two opposing Spanish factions.

A somewhat surprising side of frontier life, especially in view of our current stereotypes, is the frequency with which frontiersmen appealed to the law. Movies have given us a view of the woodsman as always ready to settle his quarrels with gun or fist at the slightest provocation. It is surprising, then, to see the settler going to the law instead. Audubon suffered from this law fever as much as his neighbors. A very trivial (but also quite typical) example of his frequent legal altercations was the lawsuit he undertook against a coon hunter in 1814. From the records we learn that he had made a deal with an unnamed trapper to procure one hundred raccoon skins. The hunter, a man from the Indiana side of the river, did not make good on his bargain, and Audubon brought suit against him. In rebuttal the hunter alleged that Audubon had omitted to carry out his part of the agreement, since he had failed to lend him his coon dog as promised. The court at once ruled that Audubon must provide the dog without delay. In due time the pelts were produced and a constable brought out a bottle of whiskey and urged all parties to down some of it as a sign that there were no hard feelings. Everyone fell in with this suggestion.

A fruitless and unhappy episode in the history of the Audubons' relations with their neighbors is to be found in the story of their involvement with George Keats and his wife. Young Keats, the brother of the poet, John Keats, appeared on the western scene in 1818 with his wife Georgiana, a lower-middle-class English girl of uneven disposition and exaggerated social pretensions. Keats had turned up, like many another, in Henderson and sought out Audubon, of whom he had heard. He then made arrangements for himself and his wife to board at the Audubons' table. At first Lucy and Georgiana appeared to get along well together, and Keats and Audubon seemed fairly compatible, finding much in common. Keats admired Audubon, the American, whom he regarded as a successfully transplanted European. Audubon for his part thought the young Englishman had the makings of a good pioneer. One day he watched Keats hacking away clumsily at a log and declared forthrightly that the Englishman's persistence was worth more than his own acquired skills.

Both Audubon and Lucy assumed at the time that they could accept Keats and his wife on terms of equality, but to do so was to reckon without Georgiana's reverse snobbery. The English girl had come up from humble origins, and while she lived at the Audubon house she came to resent Lucy's good manners and refinement, which she referred to as her "stuck-up ways." Keats sided belligerently with his wife, but for a time he and Audubon remained friends and even tried to do business together.

The enterprise in question was but another of Audubon's hastily contrived schemes. The guileless naturalist was always getting himself into these adventures, which disguised themselves as serious attempts to make money. The basis of the arrangement was the supposed purchase of a boat. Details are lacking, but Audubon seems to have become its owner by attempting to collect a worthless $4,000 note that one S. A. Bowen, a hotheaded and undependable Irishman, had proffered to its builders, Prentice and Bakewell. Keats apparently had put a small amount of money into the purchase of the boat. Next, Bowen left town in the boat and headed down the river, and when Audubon went after him, Keats assumed something was being done behind his back. This was all it took to make him Audubon's implacable enemy. When the naturalist caught up with Bowen he tried to attach the boat by court order. In this he failed, and in the meantime the boat sank.

On his return to Henderson, Audubon found to his surprise that everyone involved held him responsible for the fiasco—particularly Keats, who was happy to join the hue and cry. Audubon was taken to court about the affair, and believing that he could not obtain a fair trial in Henderson County he asked for and was granted a change of venue to the Daviess County Court. The plaintiffs failed to appear there, and the case against Audubon was dismissed. But legal success was small consolation. He himself had lost money, and because his associates had also lost theirs, they were still bitter.

The villain of the piece, Mr. Bowen, in some strange way considered Audubon personally responsible for his misfortune and vowed vengeance upon him. Audubon was duly warned by his friends that Bowen was looking for him with the intention of giving him a beating, and sure enough the attack came. At the time, Audubon was carrying his right arm in a sling, the result of an accident at the mill. Luckily for him on the day in question his usually mild Lucy had insisted that he arm himself with a dagger. Thus it happened that he was not totally unprepared for the attack. Here is Audubon's account of the affair: "As I was walking toward the steam mill one morning, I heard myself hailed from behind; on turning I observed Mr. Bowen marching towards me with a heavy club in his hand. I stood still and as soon as he reached me he complained of my conduct in New Orleans and suddenly raising his bludgeon laid it about me. Though white with wrath, I neither spoke nor moved not till he had given me twelve severe blows, then drawing my dagger with my left hand, I stabbed him and instantly he fell."

At this point an angry mob of so-called witnesses unaccountably blamed Audubon for what had happened and pursued him down the road. Bowen was too tough or too lucky to die of his wound, and on recovery he sued Audubon for assault and battery. When the case came to trial, the judge obviously enjoyed pronouncing his decision from the bench. After he dismissed the case against Audubon, he came down into the courtroom and said to him: "Mr. Audubon, you committed a serious offense,—an exceedingly serious offense, Sir,—in failing to kill the damned rascal!"

For reasons that are not quite clear, Keats and his wife continued to side against Audubon throughout the boat controversy and its aftermath and never had a good word to say for him afterwards. There was absolutely no evidence that Audubon had shown anything but good faith, but the Englishman's mind was made up and he refused to change it. He was also getting bored with life in Henderson and its few distractions, and so he sent his wife and infant daughter Emily to live in the house of Thomas Bakewell in Louisville. Then following close upon their heels George Keats himself went to Louisville and borrowed money from Bakewell for a trip to London. It is of further interest to note that Thomas Bakewell, who was indebted to Audubon morally if not financially for past favors, including two fruitless partnerships largely engineered by himself, seems to have made no attempt to defend his brother-in-law against Keats's unfounded slanders.

The whole steamboat affair was in reality a tempest in a teapot, and if anyone was the real loser it was Audubon himself, though he had not been at fault. But from the interest taken in the affair by George's famous brother, the poet John Keats, it acquired a borrowed notoriety of an extremely disagreeable character. It seems that John Keats was fed an assortment of lies by his brother and sister-in-law in Kentucky, and believed them implicitly. Then with no further knowledge of the facts he wrote the following letter to his brother George in Louisville:

I cannot help thinking Mr. Audubon a dishonest man. Why did he make you believe that he was a man of Property? How is it his circumstances have altered so suddenly? In truth, I do not believe you fit to deal with the world, or at least the American world. But, Good God!—who can avoid chances. You have done your best. Take matters as coolly as you can, and, confidently expecting help from England, act as if no help was nigh. . . . Be careful of those Americans. I could almost advise you to come, whenever you have the sum of $500 to England. Those Americans will, I am afraid, fleece you. . . . I know not how to advise you but by advising you to advise with yourself. In your next, tell me at large your thoughts about America . . . for it appears to me you have as yet been somehow deceived. I cannot help thinking Mr. Audubon has deceived you. I shall not like the sight of him. I shall endeavor to avoid seeing him.

Meanwhile Georgiana Keats allowed herself the luxury of gossiping irresponsibly and at length about Lucy Audubon to anyone who would listen. It will be remembered that she had not liked her particularly during her enforced contact with her and so, in her letters to her famous brother-in-law in England, she poured forth a torrent of gratuitous abuse. This in turn elicited from the poet another uninformed and prejudiced letter, as follows:

I was surprised to hear of the state of society in Louisville. It seems you are just as ridiculous there as we are here—three-penny parties, half-penny dances. The best thing I have heard of is your shooting. . . . Give my compliments to Mrs. Audubon and tell her I cannot think her either goodlooking or honest. Tell Mr. Audubon he's a fool. If the American ladies are worse than the English they must be very bad. You say you should like your Emily brought up here. You had better bring her up yourself. You know a good number of English ladies—what encomium could you give a half dozen of them? The greater part seem to me to be downright American. I have known more than one Mrs. Audubon. Their affectation of fashion and politeness cannot transcend ours. Look at our Cheapside sons and daughters.

Thus did John Keats's laudable desire to defend his brother and sister-in-law and to take their part against distant and, we might say, imaginary enemies, lead him to take sides in a quarrel about which he knew next to nothing. And thus was he also led to slander the good

Lucy Audubon. Fortunately for the latter's good reputation, John Keats and his sister-in-law stand virtually alone in their unflattering opinion of her. By nearly everyone else she was as dearly loved as she was sincerely admired.

# 9

# LAST DAYS IN KENTUCKY

WITHOUT A SHADOW of a doubt his last years in Kentucky were among the unhappiest of Audubon's life. Old friends were passing away. James Berthoud, for example, died in the Audubon home while on a visit there from Shippingport. The naturalist's business ventures, never under tight control, continued to crash about his head. What small profits his sales and services brought had always to go to help pay his debts. The mill was a perpetual source of difficulty. The outlook grew darker each day until at last he saw no way to raise the funds he needed except by the sale of all his assets. The pressure from his creditors grew relentless. He had been a man of status in the community. Now all that changed with his falling fortunes. As he said of his predicament: "From this date my pecuniary difficulties daily increased. I had heavy bills to pay which I could not meet or take up. The moment this became known to the world around me that moment I was assailed with thousands of invectives; the once wealthy man was now nothing."

At this juncture, when Audubon was almost desperate, Nicholas Berthoud, the son of his old friend James, came to his rescue by offering to purchase his house and its contents. The price to be paid for this portion of his property was $7,000 and what was included is described in the records. The inventory is as follows: "All houses, outhouses, rents, profits thereon, and all paintings, drawings, household and kitchen furniture and utensils in said house, houses and outhouses, stables, smithe house and storehouse in possession of said John Audubon and Lucy his wife."

We know that the inventory also included a piano, one hundred fifty books, four mirrors, twenty Windsor chairs, rugs, carpets, "diverse" furniture, china and Lucy's wedding silver. It is interesting to note that afterwards in New Orleans, with his first sizable commission for a painting, Audubon sent Lucy a complete set of queensware, and that by painting later in England the large picture *Spaniel Surprising English Pheasants*, he obtained enough money to replace the forfeited wedding silver. The replacement, consisting of a dozen and a half of each piece of the set, cost one hundred guineas.

The bitterest blow of all in this financial disaster must have been the inclusion of his paintings among his more mundane assets. But we may fairly assume that Berthoud made a gift of these to his friend subsequent to the sale. When he left Kentucky, soon afterward, Audubon speaks of his paintings as among the only assets saved from his total loss. Without these the artist would have been bereft of what he valued most.

The total sum owed to Audubon from the purchasers of his goods and properties in Henderson came to approximately $40,760, but it must be surmised that he never received anything like that much money. It would have mattered little if he had. His creditors took everything. In fact even after he left Henderson, having presumably satisfied his creditors to the best of his ability, using for the purpose every last cent of the cash realized by his forced sale, he continued to be harassed by an endless series of small lawsuits as various claimants adopted legal expedients to collect additional sums of money from him. These miscellaneous debts, still remaining, were in the neighborhood of $8,000. From this burden there was no easy relief, and so, pushed beyond endurance, he allowed himself to be jailed for debt in Louisville as a means of temporary relief from persecution. He gained his freedom shortly thereafter, but the experience must have been anything but pleasant. Subsequently he took advantage of a new Kentucky statute on bankruptcy and by going through this painful process in the courts he freed himself at last of debt and was able to make a new start financially.

As was frequently to be the case during Audubon's later wanderings, he was forced at this time to improvise a temporary modus vivendi for his family. In the Henderson area the Rankins had long been his port of storm for Lucy and the boys. Along with most of the Audubons' friends they considered themselves fortunate to procure Lucy's services as a tutor for their children. Few women of her intelligence and education were to be found on the frontier. In this position she was well able to support the two boys. But her period of full-time breadwinning had not yet arrived, and as Audubon left Henderson for Louisville in 1819, it was for the purpose of looking for work.

Audubon was confident that he was at last leaving his debts behind him, but he was quite without plans or resources for the future as he started on his three-day walk to Louisville. In his own words: "I paid all I could and left Henderson, poor and miserable in thoughts." A further proof of his despondency can be read from this protest, which seems to come from the very heart of the man: "This was the only time in my life when the wild turkeys that so often crossed my path and the thousands of lesser birds that enlivened the woods and the prairies, all looked like enemies, and I turned my eyes from them, as if I could have wished that they never existed."

When Audubon reached Louisville he found refuge for a while in the bosom of the Berthoud family in Shippingport, and from this base he sought employment. His only hope was to find a way to use one of the three skills that he had: painting, taxidermy, or merchandising. But he needed his family with him. Going it alone was always bearable for Audubon when fortune smiled, but when a mood of despair was upon him he required the presence of Lucy and the boys to help him recover his equanimity. Fortunately the generosity of Mr. Isham Talbot, a friend in Henderson, provided Lucy and the boys with a carriage, and his family was soon able to join him.

For the next few months Audubon was quite unsuccessful in his attempts to find work. From the material point of view he had reached the nadir of his existence, and the spiritual resources that he possessed in quantity were not for the moment available to enable him to overcome his gloom. He was by nature an optimist, as we have seen, but he had a practical strain too, and this demanded satisfaction. He was also proud, and although he had no objection whatever to accepting the hospitality of his friends, accustomed as he had been for some time to dealing out such hospitality himself, he knew very well that a means would soon have to be found for supporting himself and his family. For the moment he temporized and even appeared to indulge himself in his hobbies—a stance that Nicholas Berthoud found annoying. He was painting constantly, but only in a desultory way, and he gave away the results to his friends and family. But there was no possibility of hiding his worries from Lucy, for he was actually all but obsessed by them. Her own well-meant attempts to lighten her husband's spirits were not very successful either. She was pregnant at the time and the prospect of another mouth to feed was a frightening one for both parents. When Lucy was delivered of this daughter, they named her Rose; but the baby was unwell and, like her sister, seemed not likely to survive infancy.

At length as a last resort, feeling strongly that his period of total dependence on his friends must come abruptly to an end, Audubon turned seriously to his art to escape outright destitution. All he had ever cared to paint was wildlife, but in his moment of need he resolutely laid aside his hopes and ill-defined plans for the future and tried to make of his painting a means of livelihood. As he put it, addressing himself to his sons: "At last I resorted to my poor talents to maintain you and your dear mother, who fortunately became easy at her change of condition and gave me a spirit such as I really needed to meet the surly looks and cold reception of those who so shortly before were pleased to call me their friend."

Audubon worked up to his employment as an artist by easy stages, first painting without compensation the portraits of personages about town. Next he did portraits of strangers for five dollars each. His next thought was that he might obtain pupils for art lessons, and to this end he advertised in the *Western Courier,* announcing that he would give lessons in drawing and do portraits. The response of the public was slow, but after he had accomplished a few satisfactory portraits his reputation spread by word of mouth and his clientele grew. His adventures as a portrait painter were sometimes bizarre. He relates that he was frequently rushed to a bedside to paint the likeness of the dead or dying, and adds that on one occasion a child's body was exhumed so that he might paint its portrait. In the minutes that remained to him after giving lessons to children, and after gazing at the faces of those who could afford his portraits, he still managed to find time, or perhaps it should be said that he could not manage *not* to find time, to continue his nature studies and to paint birds.

In the midst of these struggles to keep his head above water, occasional lawsuits continued to plague him. There was even one undertaken in the name of his father-in-law, William Bakewell (instituted without doubt by the implacable Rebecca Smith Bakewell), to recover the sum of $5,000 supposedly due from a long previous and now forgotten debt. And as if these burdens were not enough, his young daughter Rose sickened and died and was buried in Louisville in a "lost grave," as Audubon remarked pathetically.

A lesser man would have been prostrated by the persistence of his misfortunes. Not Audubon. His brief success as an art teacher and portrait painter had heartened him again. In his autobiographical sketch he wrote thus about his darkest days:

One morning, while all of us were sadly desponding, I took you both, Victor and John, from Shippingport to Louisville. I had purchased a loaf of bread and some apples; before we reached Louisville you were all hungry, and by the riverside we sat down and ate our scanty meal. On that day the world was to me as a blank, and my heart was sorely heavy, for I scarcely had enough to keep my dear sons alive; and yet through those dark days I was being led to the development of the talents I loved. . . . I never for a day gave up listening to the songs of our birds, or watching their peculiar habits, or delineating them in the best way I could. Nay, during my deepest troubles I frequently would wrench myself from the persons around me, and retire to some secluded spot of our noble forests.

The period of art lessons and successful portrait painting was fine while it lasted, and Audubon was able to rent a house for his family in a quiet part of town. Unfortunately this comparative freedom from want was short-lived and Audubon was again reduced to penury.

It was at this low point in his affairs that he obtained an ill-starred post as a taxidermist for the Western Museum Society of Cincinnati at a salary of $125 a month. The fact that he applied for and accepted the post at all speaks volumes for his state of mind. He loathed the very thought of this work, which would keep him indoors and which provided no escape from its dull routine during business hours. He and Lucy had to be content with living in a second-rate boardinghouse, and she, pessimistic about the future, advertised for and found a teaching position. Audubon went to work, performing his chores as best he could, dreaming the while of a better future. The present reality was most discouraging, not least of all because the museum paid his salary with shocking irregularity. How long Audubon could have stood the job we do not know, for at the end of April 1820, when the museum collection was nearly complete, the director resolved some of his own financial troubles by dismissing Audubon, though promising him the payment of his arrears in salary.

The time that Audubon spent at the museum need not be considered totally lost, as he himself admitted, for during his financially unprofitable engagement there he had a chance to meet and talk to Major Long, leader of an expedition to the Rocky Mountains. When Long and his associates saw and praised Audubon's birds, at once his dormant wish to make something useful and important of his collection of bird portraits struck him again, this time with unusual force. He knew that being a portraitist for casual sitters and working as a taxidermist was not the way to realize his dream. He would have to reach a decision about the future. He was aided in his thinking by a long speech made by his employer, Dr. Drake, at which he and Lucy were present. After praising the ornithological work of Alexander Wilson, Drake mentioned Audubon by name and noted that his portfolios contained many birds that Wilson had missed. This remark gave food for thought.

After some reflection Audubon and his wife came to a serious decision. Henceforth their common goal would be his continued study and painting of birds, with a view to publishing the results. His work would be greater than Wilson's. Lucy for her part would encourage him to travel widely in the United States seeking new specimens. She would remain for the time being in Cincinnati, teaching and attempting to collect her husband's arrears in salary at the museum. Audubon would head down the Mississippi, all but penniless, and with no specific employment goal in mind except for such money as he could make by doing portraits, teaching art, and performing related odd jobs. His main effort would be directed toward filling the gaps in his portraits of American birds. For the first time in his life he would be able to devote himself to bird study without the guilty feeling that he was indulging a hobby and neglecting more serious business. Surplus, if any, he would of course send to his family, but the solid basis of financial stability would rest for the time being on Lucy's shoulders. If he had twinges of conscience at this time it was not because he was shirking his work but because the burdens that he so disliked had been shifted to his wife.

As part of his preparation for his journey he sought letters from prominent persons, among them Henry Clay. The latter replied with a useful but general letter in which he said, among other things, "I have the satisfaction of personal acquaintance with Mr. John J. Audubon, and I have learned from others who have known him longer and better that his character and conduct have been uniformly good." Clay then commended him to officers of the United States government whom he might meet. William Henry Harrison also wrote a letter in his behalf recommending him to the military commander of the post at the fork of the Arkansas River. With these documents and a few others with which he provided himself Audubon was ready to carry out his plan.

When arrangements between husband and wife had been concluded, they were undoubtedly looked upon as temporary, for in the nineteenth century women were seldom regarded as wage earners. There is reason to believe also that Lucy's family took a dim view of the course on which her husband had embarked. Letters from Philadelphia were curt and usually dealt with money matters, especially with Audubon's failure to acquit himself of all his debts. Local friends were also impatient with him. The self-righteous but generally helpful Nicholas Berthoud thought Audubon had frittered away his substance in Henderson and for this reason did not come to his old friend's aid. Although he must have known that he and Audubon were setting out for New Orleans at about the same time, he did not offer him passage on his boat and from his vantage point of comfort and affluence took it upon himself to criticize Audubon for his shortcomings at this time of misfortune.

When the day finally came to leave Cincinnati, Audubon took passage in a nondescript riverboat loaded with equally nondescript passengers. His only companion was a promising boy named Mason, of whom he proposed to make an artist—a plan that was to turn out badly. Husband and wife separated lovingly but with grave misgivings.

Two-thirds of the way down the river, when Audubon and Berthoud chanced to meet in Natchez, the latter had second thoughts about his selfishness as he slept comfortably in a hotel room while Audubon was out on the riverbank, wrapped in a blanket. At this point he invited Audubon and Mason to continue their trip to New Orleans in his boat.

Audubon's valedictory to the years of success, failure and struggle in Kentucky is contained in a pair of entries in his diary:

*Nov. 2, 1820. Floated down slowly within two miles of Henderson. I can scarcely conceive that I stayed there eight years, and passed therein comfortably, for it is undoubtedly on the poorest spot in the country according to my present opinion.*

*Nov. 3, 1820. We left our anchor at daybreak, and passed Henderson about sunrise. I looked on the mill, perhaps for the last time, and with thoughts that almost made my blood run cold bade it an eternal farewell.*

These were harsh words, but they hardly represent a considered opinion. They were rather the spontaneous outpouring of a man still tied to his misfortune. Far more significant a measure of his deeper feelings is the fact that in the tranquility of later life, the Kentucky years were singled out for affectionate mention and recollection. Victor and John he always called "my Kentucky boys," and Kentucky remained for him a chosen land, the best land he had known.

# 10

## EPILOGUE

WHEN IN 1820 John James and Lucy Audubon made the hard decision to separate for a while so that he might pursue his nature studies on the Mississippi and in the southern states while she remained with their sons in Cincinnati, they were deciding more than they knew. Audubon's life was about half over. The second half of that life was to bear little resemblance to the first. In the hotel in Louisville and the log houses in Henderson, whether actually the property of the Audubons or not, the family had always had a home together. Now for many years to come Audubon and Lucy were to have no home to call their own. Lucy would be living principally with the families whose children she was tutoring, with friends or, later on, traveling about from great house to hotel in England and elsewhere while her husband pursued his goal of publishing his great work. This meant, among other things, that she would no longer be running the equivalent of a boardinghouse in Henderson where her husband's friends and acquaintances came and went and took their meals. If Lucy became by her new post a wage earner she was also, from this time forth, free of the drudgery of housework.

For Audubon his new freedom meant, though he could not have known it either, that he would no longer have to make half-hearted attempts to earn a living as a merchant, with no time for painting and nature study other than what he could manage to take from the hours he was supposed to spend on the chores of storekeeping. It meant for man and wife that for a considerable period of time the children would be raised by Lucy. Audubon was most of the time long gone and far gone.

Most marriages would be hard put to endure under such conditions, and that of the Audubons was no exception. We know from the correspondence between John James and Lucy that once or twice misunderstandings, caused presumably by little more than absence itself, but complicated by money problems, near-failure, and the psychological maladjustments that such worries caused, came close to destroying the relationship between them. Yet in the end affection won out. They stayed together and loved each other well in spite of all. When Audubon's great triumph finally came with the gradual publication from 1827 to 1838 of the *Birds of America*, the victory over adversity, which among lesser persons might have meant the doom of their affection, became instead the cornerstone of the happy marriage of their later years.

The farewell to Kentucky written during the trip down the Mississippi River in the year 1820 implied that henceforth Audubon's whereabouts would be hard to predict. He might be anywhere in North America or Western Europe. He generally considered his wanderings profitable, for he was finding and sketching many unfamiliar species. For this reason when he wrote home he generally did so in a cheerful vein. He found it hard to understand why Lucy, who did not possess the intense joie de vivre that his talent gave him, wrote to him less frequently and less enthusiastically about her life as a teacher. Little wonder then that Lucy and her husband looked back later to the days in Henderson and Louisville as the happy years of their married life. They had been young and struggling, but they had been together.

The Audubons had not seen Kentucky for the last time. Returning from Louisiana two years later, and leaving

Lucy to continue her teaching on a plantation, Audubon took Victor to Kentucky and apprenticed him to Nicholas Berthoud. Instead of remaining there but briefly, as he had planned, Audubon was forced to stay several months until the ice broke up on the river. When he did leave, in April, he went to Pittsburgh in a steamboat, a slightly more luxurious form of travel than he had previously enjoyed.

Some years later, after four years spent in England promoting the sale of the *Birds of America,* he was back in Louisville again for a happy reunion with old friends. And yet once again, in 1843, he came to the city, and this time its citizens, among whom were many old friends and acquaintances, tendered him a banquet. On this festive occasion he was acclaimed a great man, for his reputation as a naturalist had spread far and wide. He was by then a published author and a member of learned academies. After the banquet he visited with his old friend Mrs. Gwathmey, widow of his friend the proprietor of the Indian Queen. He also spent a day with Lucy's younger brother, William Bakewell. And contrary to his prediction, his trip took him past the town of Henderson, where the ugly old mill stood as if to mock him.

On this last visit to Louisville and vicinity Audubon perceived all too well that his beloved woods were fast disappearing. He saw like an Orwell of his day that the future was not necessarily so bright as Americans thought it must inevitably be. He remarked thoughtfully and regretfully: "Our union, instead of being in a state of nature, is now more or less covered with villages, farms and towns, where the din of the hammer and machinery is constantly heard. . . . the woods are disappearing fast under the axe by day and by fire at night, hundreds of steamboats are gliding to and fro over the whole length of the majestic river forcing commerce to take root and to prosper at every spot; when I see the surplus population of Europe coming to assist in the destruction of the forest and transplant civilization into its darkest recesses; when

I remember that these extraordinary changes have taken place in the short period of twenty years, I pause, I wonder, and although I know all to be a fact, can scarcely believe its reality."

After this last, most memorable visit to Kentucky, Audubon went east with a heart full of gratitude for the kindness of his fellow Kentuckians, and for the rest of his life, whenever he wished to honor a guest at his table in his Hudson River home, it was his custom to say: "I'll give you a real Kentucky dinner."

After the death of her husband in New York on January 27, 1851, Lucy Bakewell Audubon returned to Louisville with her granddaughter Harriet. She moved to Shelbyville shortly thereafter and lived with relatives until her death in 1874. Harriet Audubon, known as Miss Hattie, was for many years a schoolteacher in Louisville. She died in 1934.

Audubon belongs to all of America, but Kentucky's claim upon him as an adopted son is without question. He is to be reckoned among her great men.